HOTEL AND RESTAURANT DESIGN
Douglas Smith

VNR VAN NOSTRAND REINHOLD COMPANY
NEW YORK   CINCINNATI   TORONTO   LONDON   MELBOURNE

Hotel and Restaurant Design
Published in the United Kingdom 1978
by Design Council
28 Haymarket, London SW1Y 4SU

Published in the United States of America by
Van Nostrand Reinhold Company
A Division of Litton Educational Publishing, Inc
450 West 33rd Street, New York, New York 10001, USA

Van Nostrand Reinhold Limited
1410 Birchmount Road, Scarborough,
Ontario M1P 2E7, Canada

Printed and bound in the United Kingdom by
Hazell Watson & Viney Ltd
Aylesbury, Bucks

Copyright © 1978 by Douglas Smith
Library of Congress Catalog Card #77-90841

ISBN 0-442-27795-4

16 15 14 13 12 11 10 9 8 7 6 5 4 3 2 1

Introduction

The aim of this book is to stimulate good design in hotels and restaurants, whether the design problem is a small alteration to existing premises, a larger extension, or the planning of a completely new building.

In particular, the book is intended to help owners and operators of small and medium-sized hotels and restaurants to improve the services they offer and the places in which they offer them. Good design pays in these matters by suggesting ways of improving buildings and equipment to increase efficiency and, as a result, profitability. As the surroundings become more attractive, so the demand for accommodation increases. Careful planning and imagination will realise the potential of a building to the full, whether it is new or old.

The book has therefore been written as a comprehensive guide to the design of hotels, motels, restaurants and snack bars. Many of the design principles discussed will be common to most projects and the book is structured to be as easy to use as possible for a wide range of different problems, from starting with a vacant building site to the redesign of a single room. It is divided into sections that deal with different aspects of the subject, but these are, of course, interdependent and they are intended to interact to suggest as many ideas as possible to the reader.

The hotel and catering industry in Britain is under considerable pressure to improve its facilities, largely because of the direct comparison that can now be made by many people who have tasted the fruits of catering in other countries through package holidays. In fact, the publication of the *Guide Michelin* to Great Britain and Ireland in 1974 meant that, for the first time, direct parallels could be drawn between the British industry and its counterparts abroad. No operator can afford to ignore the demands that have resulted from what, in general, has been an unfavourable comparison.

Good design and imaginative planning create the right effect at the right costs. This book is not intended

Extremes of scale. Above, a large modern hotel near a national landmark. Below, a small restaurant in a Regency town.

to replace the professional designer, although it should enable the small owner or manager to carry out some plans himself. It is equally important that the hotelier and the designer should each understand the other's problems and approaches, so that the final solution satisfies their needs and those of the public. The book should help here to bridge the gap.

DOUGLAS SMITH

4

1 PLANNING

Planning philosophy

A fundamental change has taken place in recent years in the public's relationship with hotels, restaurants and the catering trade in general. Higher living standards, increased personal mobility and cheap travel overseas have introduced a vast number of people of widely differing backgrounds to the industry. There is a demand for higher standards at competitive prices and comparisons can be freely made between British and Continental practice. Gone are the days when visitors readily accepted a shared bathroom, and small hotels now face the problem of competing with large chain operations that offer good standards of accommodation at competitive rates. At the lower end of the market, cheap cafés have to consider the growing challenge offered to them by the increasing number of specialist snack bars and foreign restaurants.

In all this, there is a challenge to management and designers alike to carry out some fundamental thinking and produce long-term strategies that will allow short-term decisions to be made efficiently and without prejudicing the future. Large hotel and catering groups will be able to carry out an extensive research programme; the smaller operation can achieve similar results by following the same guidelines and by inspiration. But the wrong facilities, however good they may be, will never be a success. Hotels and restaurants are for people and they must provide a service. If this service is out of tune with what is needed in a particular area at a given time then the operation is bound to be a failure. If in doubt, go back and consider the clientele.

This suggests the need for constant monitoring of the operation. Management must always be reviewing the demand, for it will never be static and it is essential to respond to changes by introducing new ideas, while retaining the best of the old. The mobile society of which we are part has changed its eating habits and there is a growing demand for better and more interesting foods – including exotic ones. Unfortunately, however, the design of restaurants and smaller eating places still does not receive the attention it deserves. The catering trade could take greater advantage of the potential offered by such a basic human need.

The feasibility study

As a first step in developing or establishing a hotel or restaurant, a feasibility study should be undertaken to establish the type and level of accommodation that should be provided. Costs will have to be compared with the anticipated occupancy rates and the type of clientele. A commercial hotel that has little opportunity to attract weekend trade will force management to make different decisions than would be the case for a holiday hotel, for example. The functions may be combined in another situation, where seventy to eighty per cent occupancy might be the aim.

Such a feasibility study could be carried out under the following headings, which can be given more or less emphasis as required:

Type of premises, hotel, motel, restaurant or snack bar
Grade of premises, set against the pattern of establishments in the area, paying special attention to any gaps in the market
Occupancy, short or long stay, weekend or weekday trade
Clientele, regular visitors or casual trade
Cost of meals and room rates, set against expected demand and prices charged within the area
Extension provisions, to cope with future demand and changing requirements
Interior type and quality
Traffic analysis
Town planning, available information on strategy planning and detail plans that could affect the scheme
Communications, private and public transport by rail, road and air
Economic development, study the plan for the area, if any
Local potential, historic, architectural, scenic and cultural
Available finance, how much and in what form
Staff availability, together with accommodation and transport requirements
Site planning, if a new site is required this must be discussed with estate agents and the local authority but the design team should be involved at a very early stage

The cost plan

A cost plan must be used by the design team in order to achieve maximum results within a controlled budget. What is needed is a careful balance of expenditure between each element of the building, its planning, structure, materials and finishes so as to achieve the best value for money. The overall impression that the building will make on the clientele must be taken into consideration and a conscious decision may have to be made to spend more money on one part of the scheme at the expense of another. Whereas the initial feasibility study should produce a total budget cost, the cost plan will ensure that the best possible building is arrived at

within the budget and give a breakdown of costs for each part of the project. Building costs will be only a part of the total cost, which can be broken down under the following headings:

Site costs
Construction costs
Furnishing costs
Equipment costs
Graphics costs
Fees
Financial costs, including bridging loans
Advertising costs
Insurance

A proportion should be added to the total cost to take care of unforeseen emergency payments. This contingency sum might be 5 to 10 per cent of the total.

The design team can help to assess the different parts of the feasibility study and cost plan. The earlier they are involved, the clearer and more decisive the resulting design brief will be.

The design brief

A properly analysed, clear and well defined design brief is essential, whether work is to be carried out by appointing an independent designer or solving the problem internally. Time spent setting out the objectives and detail requirements for the project will save both money and time later on and is the most cost effective way of tackling the problem. The resulting design brief can be written, drawn, or a combination of both. It should cover the following areas, many of which will have emerged from ideas produced at the stage of the feasibility study:

Type of establishment required
Size, including type and number of rooms
Flexibility, consider double rooms in place of single ones
Eating facilities, including type of service and food
Other facilities, including conferences
Ancillary areas, showcases, shops
Type of service
Site location, treatment and transport facilities
Costs, taking into account capital and running costs
Profitability, resulting from a market survey of possible charging rates

Basic principles of planning

Different types of establishment will naturally require different approaches to their design. This raises the question of definitions. In some people's minds, for example, there is a fundamental difference between a hotel and a motel, but much confusion has arisen in practice with the introduction of the motor hotel.

A motel, in the strict definition, is essentially a hotel designed for motorists who want to park their car close to their rooms and use the bedrooms for more than just a sleeping capsule. Experience suggests that freedom of use is essential. Rooms can be vacated early and it is probably best to arrange payment on arrival rather than departure, with cash payment for extra facilities without billing and a large number of do-it-yourself facilities – from early morning tea-makers to vending machines. Hotels are less dominated by the car, and the degree of luxury and the balance of self-help and service will depend upon the type and grade of establishment. It will therefore be important to establish the type of facilities to be provided and the likely clientele in addition to all the other requirements in the design brief.

Motor hotels to some extent bridge the gap between hotels and motels, but the cars need not be parked very close to rooms. They will probably be organised along the same lines as the motel, with visitors paying for food and drink directly and being charged for their room on arrival.

Restaurants and snack bars require a totally different approach, which is considered in greater detail in Section 5. It is still essential, however, to establish the likely clientele and the nature of the building. The design team should exploit to the full any particular design element associated with the type of food provided. First impressions of the establishment are likely to be very important and will directly affect its appeal. A snack bar with the appearance of a luxury restaurant will not satisfy the users' needs. The implications in terms of capital costs will probably make prices too high, and the finishes unable to withstand hard wear.

COMMUNICATION PATTERNS IN HOTELS AND MOTELS

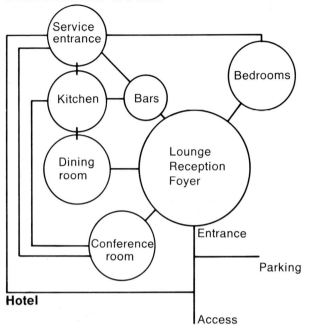

Hotel

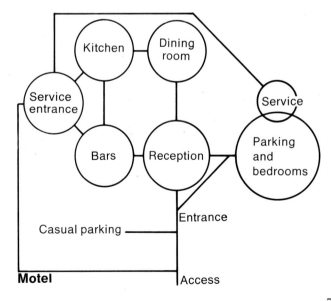

Motel

The plan-form

The plan-form of the building will directly affect its cost. A square or rectangular plan is the cheapest and the more complex the shape the greater the cost.

If an entirely new building is required there will be relatively few restrictions on its external form. The plan can then be established after consideration of the natural features of the site. Existing buildings will affect the plan to a greater or lesser extent, but it is essential to carry out a fundamental appraisal of the scheme to establish its main objectives. It may be that making a structural alteration, or reconsidering some feature, will improve the plan and produce a more satisfactory solution. Any decision should be related directly to the function of the scheme as a whole.

At the two extremes of the range of possible solutions are the open and closed plan-forms. In an open plan all facilities, with the exception of bedrooms, are provided in a single space in which areas for different activities are separated and defined by screens, furniture and, perhaps, changes of level in floors and ceilings. The result is a fluid plan that can be modified quickly and easily to suit changing needs. A considerable amount of money will have to be spent on providing sufficiently flexible services, including acoustic insulation, and the total area may have to be relatively large in order to have adequate divisions between the various functions.

The closed plan, in which each function is contained in a separate room, requires little explanation, although it needs careful planning for maximum efficiency and convenience. The open and closed plan-forms can be successfully merged in a single scheme. Extreme examples of either of them are only likely to apply to a few buildings.

The function of the building needs to be studied very carefully to avoid possible conflict between the circulation of staff and the circulation of the clientele. Priorities must be established; staff fatigue is important in that it will affect efficiency, the staff's reaction to guests and the calibre of staff who can be recruited. The correct positioning of rooms and the relationship between them should also be closely considered in the light of providing services for the building. Where possible, centralisation of services such as bathrooms within the

plan should be aimed at on cost grounds, reducing not only capital costs but, equally important, running costs later on.

PLAN FORMS
Open plan hotel

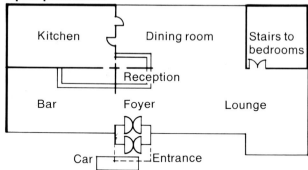

Closed plan hotel

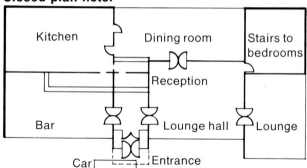

Motel

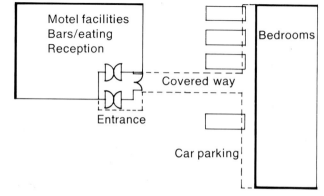

The site

The site is an important part of any scheme and should be looked at in terms of its intrinsic qualities (contour and landscape), its position relative to transport facilities, and any other amenities it provides, such as scenic views.

Decisions on access should be taken early on, remembering to provide separate service areas so that guests arriving at the hotel do not have to walk past the dustbins. Noise from surrounding areas, and particularly traffic or industrial noise, should be taken into consideration. Prevailing winds will affect the positioning of rooms with opening windows and outdoor terraces. Landscaping the site can play an important part in providing the right setting and giving a good first impression to guests.

The basic shape of the building, and its height in particular, will have a fundamental effect on the overall plan. Any decisions on flexibility of use and possible expansion should be made at an early stage. The cost plan will establish the level of services that can be reasonably provided within the budget for the scheme – from simple heating installations, for example, to full air conditioning.

Existing buildings will set a challenge for the design team who will have to produce imaginative solutions that integrate the old with the new and provide facilities in an ordered manner so that, when completed, the building gives the impression of a correct relationship between rooms and minimal conflict in the structure of the building. The ideal solution is one in which the extension is not obvious.

Car parking is a major problem and the impact of vast areas of parking space must be considered, not only in detail, but in terms of its general position to minimise the effect on the building and its surroundings. The local planning department will have precise requirements for car parking. These may affect all other decisions and limit the size of the establishment.

Below, site considerations. Right, car parking

SITE FACTORS

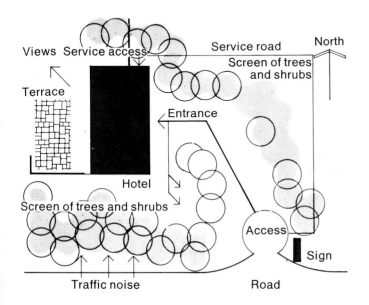

MODIFYING THE VISUAL IMPACT OF CAR PARKING

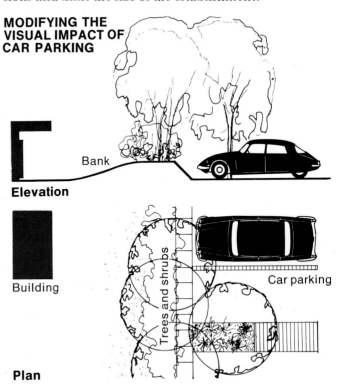

9

Sketch design

The sketch design produced by the design team following the brief resulting from the feasibility study and cost plan should be treated very much as an ideas document. To encourage the full use of the skills of the design team, and thus the best possible solution, it is best to provide a good brief but not to superimpose preconceived ideas about planning before a sketch design has been produced. It is essential to appraise and criticise the sketch plan as constructively as possible, since time spent in getting the building right at this stage will save costs by avoiding changes and delays later on, which can have catastrophic effects on both timetable and budget. A good design team will welcome and respond to constructive criticism.

It is worth sending copies of the sketch design to the local planning department, building controller, fire officer, licensing justices, police and public health authority to get their ideas and requirements at an early date. Fundamental changes can then be incorporated as the plan is developed.

Programme

It is most important for the proprietor, management and the design team to agree a programme for the entire scheme (not just the construction element) so that their efforts can be co-ordinated effectively. Such a programme should cover:

1 Inception – producing an initial statement of requirements and outlining the possible courses of action and the appointment of outside consultants
2 Feasibility study
3 Cost plan
4 Sketch design
5 Detail design
6 Production information
7 Specification and bills of quantities
8 Tender and action to completion
9 Furnishing and commissioning

SPECIMEN PROGRAMMING CHART

Programme		Job												Date	
MONTHS	Apr	May	Jun	Jul	Aug	Sep	Oct	Nov	Dec	Jan	Feb	Mar
WEEKS	1 2 3 4	5 6 7 8 9										
Appointment of design team	▨											
Feasibility study	▨▨▨											
Cost plan		▨▨										
Sketch design												
Detail design												
Production information												
Specification/bill of quantities												
Tender period												
Building programme												
Furnishing												
Commissioning												

2 THE SITE AND LANDSCAPE

Design and planning

A brief section on landscape and garden design can only serve as an introduction to a fascinating subject. For the investment it involves, landscape design will add more to the appearance and facilities of a building than any other form of work. It is hard to understand, therefore, why so little thought is given to the subject.

At its best, landscape design achieves a delicate relationship between plants and the hard materials that surround them. Bare soil is the enemy of good design in this context; it also leads to high maintenance costs as the gardener is perpetually forced to fight against the growth of weeds.

The first step in designing and planning from the landscape point of view is to assess the potential of the site, its natural features and existing planting. The requirements of the landscape must be analysed, looking in turn at the function of each part of the site and setting criteria for each in the same way as for planning the interior of a building. Different areas will be set aside for privacy, for eating, for relaxation and recreation, for car parking, for services and for other utilitarian purposes. The setting of the buildings in the landscape, the view of and from the site, and the use of plant material then complete and enhance the project.

The existing levels of the site must be considered in the light of landscape, and practical requirements and modifications made as necessary. A small change of level so that the ground falls naturally into different areas can make a fantastic difference to the appearance of the site: a sloping site, for example, must be slightly remodelled if water is to be introduced so that a natural-looking basin for water to collect can be provided, otherwise it will appear artificial and uncomfortable.

Car parking and sports areas such as tennis courts can be unsightly features, but with a little imagination and slight moulding of ground levels they can be made insignificant from the main vantage points of rooms in the buildings or from terraces, and they can be concealed further if necessary by planting. Outdoor sitting areas are well worth having, as they considerably extend the usable area of the building. Internal spaces can, in effect, flow out into the landscape to form a pleasant extension for the clientele. No space is too small to be considered: the Japanese can produce a fascinating garden within the space of a square metre or two, with carefully selected paving, plants, and perhaps a thimbleful of water.

The elements of surprise and illusion can be used with great success in this area, and careful screening of certain parts of the garden from general view with a path that winds its way into these areas can give an interesting effect. In small gardens the illusion of distance can be created by using strong-coloured plants and flowers close to the building or terrace, with blue-green plant shades further away. In overall design terms a simple, clear solution that contrasts a carefully shaped lawn with shrubs and plants will reduce maintenance costs and also provide an excellent setting for the building itself.

Hard landscape

Hard landscape is the name given to extensions of the building such as drives, terraces, paths, walls and steps. Careful consideration should be given to their design as part of the design of the building, and some continuity between the various elements should be the aim. A sensitive approach to hard landscape is equally important in the case of old buildings.

Terraces are a particularly important feature of the hard landscape in the case of hotels. They can be sited either adjacent to the building or away from it, depending on the requirements of the site, the position of the buildings in relation to the sun and the prevailing winds. A terrace must be sufficiently large to enable chairs to be grouped round tables; the narrow strip so frequently seen along the side of a building provides very little useful space.

Surface textures are a particularly important feature of terraces and paths, and a decision will have to be taken on what quality to provide. The photographs show a selection of materials and combinations of these can be used. Using natural materials over a very large area can be expensive, but it is possible to use a combination in which such materials are emphasised to produce a similar effect.

The quality of existing landscape and garden features, together with those of the surrounding area as a whole, must be taken into consideration when deciding on the design of, and materials for, the external landscape. Apart from its relation to the building that it surrounds, the landscape of the site will come into close contact with the natural landscape and with other, nearby buildings. In this case, and particularly in a conservation area or an area of outstanding natural beauty or architectural merit, a sensitive approach to planning and design is essential.

Terraces and outdoor sitting areas can be made more attractive in certain instances by the use of some form of frame or enclosure. There are many types worth consideration, from a totally enclosed roof to a few slats of timber or the shade of a tree. If trees are used in this way it is important to consider both the amount of light that can penetrate and the problem of drips from leaves. In the case of large trees, rain can drip from leaves long after a storm has ended, and certain trees drop sticky substances or attract insects. On the other hand, trees provide a particularly attractive shade on hot summer days as the branches and leaves seem to generate some movement of air even when there is little or no wind.

Features such as sculpture or garden ornaments can be considered either as part of the hard landscape or as part of the soft landscape of vegetation, which will be considered in the next section. Any well chosen piece of sculpture, or a simple bowl-shaped plant container, can act as a focal point in an outside space.

Left, a carefully designed, but informal, path through a wild garden. Below, plants and structures enclosing an interesting space

Top, left to right, granite and cobbles set in no-fines concrete, contrasting cobbles and interlocking brick. Second row, different textures in brick and granite setts. Third row, cobbles in various patterns. Bottom, paving stones contrasting with loose gravel, stone steps, wood paving

Opposite, contrasting forms and textures of water, sand, rocks and plants

Opposite, although their styles differ, all these areas show the effect of careful detailing and a clear idea of the effect they should achieve

Above, this beautiful garden creates illusions, rhythms and movement by an interesting land form, trained vegetation and features concealed from view from various positions

A naturalised fern gulley in which a specimen tree contrasts with the natural community of plants

Soft landscape

The soft landscape comprises the grass and herb layer which the eye passes over; the shrub layer with which the eye is constantly in contact; and the tree layer which dominates the scene and can be used as a canopy, as a frame for distant views, or simply as a large, three-dimensional feature in the landscape.

In Britain, where conditions for plant growth are generally good, the choice of plants of all types is very extensive. Many problems may perhaps be the result of there being too wide a choice. Two essential assessments must be made before any choice of plants is made. The first of these is the type of soil on the site and, in particular, its acidity. By far the greater number of trees and shrubs succeed equally well on both chalky and non-chalky soils. There are, however, a few species that are lime-haters, and the following should usually be avoided on soils containing free lime or chalk: heathers and ericas, rhododendrons, azaleas, Douglas fir and yew. For a comprehensive list it is best to consult a standard reference book, such as *Trees and Shrubs*, by W J Bean. The second assessment is that of studying the natural community of plant life in the area in order to select the dominant plant types, including larger trees and shrubs.

It is essential to choose plants that will grow easily and well, so taking both the soil and the existing, natural vegetation into account will provide a useful starting point for design. It is much more important to have plants that will grow properly than to have exotic plants that take enormous amounts of time and trouble but never do well. On the other hand, the use of one or two unusual plants not from the natural community list will provide a highlight and sparkle to the overall design if they are chosen carefully.

It is impossible, in a short space, to cover all the points that should be considered when drawing up a planting plan for a site. The grouping of plants is particularly important, however, in that by using the same plants together the group will assume the identity of the individual type of plant, but at the same time achieve a correct sense of scale in relation to the landscape. This is much more effective when similar varieties are grouped together; it is essential to avoid different types of plant next to one another dotted over

Trees used to frame a view

Contrast of form in planting

the whole landscape. Bold groupings of different sizes, with some isolated specimens of individual plants, will give the best quality to the design.

Another important consideration, apart from the general texture, colour, form and size of plants, is their appearance throughout the year. Too much emphasis is often placed on flowering plants that, in many cases, only look their best for two or three weeks in each year. Generally speaking, the smaller the garden the more attention must be paid to the precise texture, form and colour of the plants it contains.

Water

Water is an attractive element to introduce into any landscape; it contrasts beautifully with all other parts of the garden, giving a reflective surface, horizontal lines and even, in the case of cascades and fountains, visual and aural variety as well. Water increases the maintenance problems, of course, but if a pond is well designed and constructed, and carefully planted and stocked with fish and water snails, the problems of pollution and maintenance are considerably reduced. Many materials can be used for forming ponds, including plastics sheet, glass reinforced plastics, and concrete.

Water features also provide an excellent opportunity to introduce a totally different group of plants into the landscape. Most water plants grow quickly and, in fact, this is the method that provides the closest thing to an instant garden at a reasonable price.

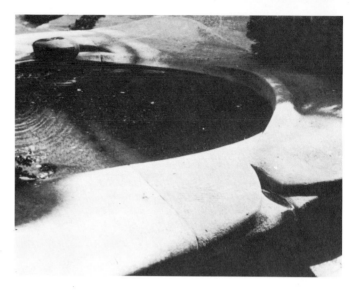

SMALL RETAINING WALLS

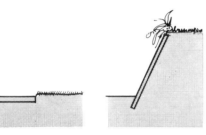
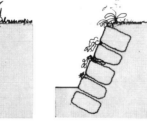

Slabs should be set 10mm below grass level

Slabs used to form small retaining wall

Correct dry stone retaining wall

Rigid heavy vehicle

11m 1.2m 7.35m 0.75m 2.45m 4.95m 7.25m

Large car

5.45m 0.9m 1.25m 3.35m 0.5m 2.75m 4.1m

Left, for occasional parking, it is possible to use special concrete paving through which grass can grow

Cars

The car provides the designer with a major problem: it is, of course, essential that guests should be able to arrive easily and without obstruction at the entrance to the building and to park their cars without difficulty. However, cars en masse are unsightly and they will detract from the quality of both the landscape and the building if they are allowed to do so. Some solution must therefore be found to minimise the effect of the car park on the landscape.

Skilful moulding of the ground, with a depression of a metre or less, can help to conceal the car park from important parts of the building and the rest of the site. It is particularly important to try and prevent cars from interrupting the horizontal view across the site. The parking area itself can be broken down by using trees and shrubs. A change of surface from the driveway to the park can provide interest and car spaces can be marked out by a change of material. Oceans of tarmac are generally very dispiriting and should be avoided if possible. Trees used in car parks must be selected to minimise the problems associated with falling leaves in autumn and should have reasonably small leaves. Trees that drop sticky substances should also be avoided. Some good choices are the manna ash, silver birch, robinia, wild cherry, ailanthus and Norway maple, to mention but a few.

3 THE BUILDINGS FROM THE OUTSIDE

The site

Guests will receive their first impressions from the appearance of the site, its development, and the external appearance of the buildings. All of these should therefore be pleasing to the eye and present an inviting look that will signal a welcome to the guests as they arrive.

The siting and landscaping of the buildings are of great importance, and landscaping has been covered in the previous section. In urban sites it is particularly necessary to consider the relationship between the buildings and their surrounding architecture.

The approach itself must be visible and clearly signed. In the case of a hotel or motel that relies on a nearby high-speed road for access, it will be necessary to attract drivers' attention well in advance of the entrance to enable them to slow down and make a safe approach, so special provision should be made for this. The access drive should be attractive and should direct guests to the main entrance to the building. From this point it should be possible to see where the car park is located without allowing it to dominate the scene. The drive must not take guests past delivery entrances, stores or dustbins as they arrive. Good facilities should be provided for taxis to unload at the entrance and it is worth considering whether to have some sort of canopy above the entrance to allow access under cover in bad weather. Adequate turning space and, where large numbers are catered for, a base for waiting taxis and coaches should be provided. In some cases, public transport will be an important element in planning this part of the facilities and easy access to, and information about, roads, railways and airports will have to be provided.

The buildings should be placed so that noise from all sources, including transport, is reduced to a minimum. This will have to be taken into account, together with the other factors of site contours, prevailing winds, sun and possible views, when deciding on the fundamental landscape design.

The separate service area should be strategically placed to give good access for large vehicles delivering supplies, fuel and stores, and also for the removal of refuse. It is important to provide adequate room for turning and a carefully designed and sited screen will hide dustbins and incinerators from view, remembering that these should be concealed both from within the buildings and from the outside grounds.

New buildings in rural areas

It is essential that, as a first step, the design team should carefully identify the quality of the countryside and assess the likely impact of new buildings on the landscape. The planning authority should be consulted at the beginning; a dialogue between the design team and the local planners will reduce the risk of misunderstandings, confrontation and delay, and will encourage the planners to respond to the project imaginatively.

In the British Isles in particular, the horizon is an important element in the landscape because the eye is attracted to the point of contrast between the light sky and the predominantly dark land mass. Buildings in rural areas should avoid breaking the horizon line when viewed from surrounding roads or countryside. Above all, consideration should be given to the scale of the project: the buildings and large areas of hard landscape associated with access drives and car parking produce major problems in a predominantly soft, rural landscape. These can be minimised by careful design of the building and strategic planting of trees and shrubs.

Any new building should have vitality and interest. The elements that go to make up the building will affect not only its external shell, but also its long-term performance and ease of maintenance. The structure itself, and all the other components of the site associated with it, must be considered from the start of the project so that materials are not used as mere decoration after the building itself has been designed. The building must be considered from both inside and outside the site, with materials chosen for their practical suitability and their compatibility with the surroundings. Clay bricks improve with age while concrete and plastics finishes tend to deteriorate; marble requires polishing; stone is good but expensive; concrete finishes need sensitive handling in the rather diffuse lighting conditions that prevail in Britain, if enough contrast is to be achieved. Windows must be considered in terms of their size related to function; large areas of window produce problems of heat gain in summer and heat loss in winter. The grouping of windows in the façade will greatly affect the overall quality of the building. The roof will be a major feature when seen from the site and the surrounding countryside, and its colour will be important.

Buildings with pitched and flat roofs can both fit into the landscape if combined with planting and sited below the skyline

The clean lines of modern buildings contrast effectively with natural elements in the landscape. Materials must be carefully chosen and detail design is important

New buildings in towns

In an old townscape site, the design team should make a careful study of the town, its architecture and the materials used in its construction. Special attention should be paid to the detail design and modelling of nearby buildings. Most old towns have a rich variety of vernacular buildings rather than one predominant style of architecture and it is best to avoid any attempt to produce a mock example of the style of an earlier period. Good, modern buildings that are sensitive to the quality of the past will provide a better solution, with appropriate detailing and choice of materials to give it the right quality for its surroundings.

The new building should contribute to the urban street scene while being woven into the urban fabric. Most sites can be linked with a particular local identity and with existing groups of buildings. The comments on the choice of materials for practicality and maintenance in the previous section on rural sites equally apply.

26

Sensibly scaled and detailed new buildings using appropriate materials are generally more successful in a townscape than copies of past styles

Old buildings

The use of existing, old buildings that need no extension or major structural alteration, but do require complete modernisation, provides a challenge to the design team. The quality of the building as it stands must be assessed, starting with the outside and considering the alterations that have taken place in the past with the introduction of new services, producing too many visible pipes and surface wiring. There is frequently a problem of accumulation, as the façade becomes hung with extra pipes and wires. When refitting the interior the opportunity can be taken to reduce these additions to a minimum. Services need particularly careful attention at ground level to avoid a multitude of pipes emerging from the walls and sloping down to open gullies. Modern back-inlet gullies and carefully sited manhole covers will help to improve the general quality of the building as seen from the outside and will provide practical advantages as well.

Years of accumulated grime can hide the intrinsic quality of old buildings and modern methods of washing, steam cleaning and grit blasting can be used to redress the situation. Cleaning methods vary according to the problem and advice should be taken before alterations are made to the interior; the grit associated with some methods can produce internal difficulties from dust, and water from washing can penetrate and harm the interior. The correct sequence of work is therefore important.

Past extensions and alterations should be carefully considered. It may be worth modifying and improving these if minor alterations and small changes here can make all the difference between success and failure of the final scheme. Any major structural work, such as repairs to roofs, walls, windows and doors, should be carried out to begin with; damp-proof courses and treatment of walls and roofs to reduce water penetration and improve insulation should be scheduled at an early stage.

Left, careful design can make the most of facilities without spoiling the environment. Below, a strikingly shaped restaurant in a London park. Opposite, floodlighting of both landscapes and buildings will add to their appeal and usefulness at night

Constrasting styles in entrances, both with a strong visual appeal

Effective floodlighting of old buildings

Right, brickwork can be cleaned with dramatic effects. Far right, exposed woodwork can be renovated. Below, a ruined castle converted into a restaurant, incorporating new materials

Extensions and conversions

Extending and converting old buildings for new uses opens up a whole range of possibilities to the designer. European Architectural Heritage Year has recently made people more aware of the need to find new uses for old buildings, and conversion to provide a hotel or restaurant is frequently a good plan for a building that has ceased to be satisfactory for its original purpose.

The scale of hotels and restaurants, and particularly large ones, can produce a challenge when, for example, converting a group of domestic buildings in the centre of a town. The problem is to combine adequate facilities while retaining the original quality and identity of the buildings, but this can usually be achieved with care and imagination. Examples are the conversion of a series of old houses in Holland into a modern hotel that retains a homely, friendly atmosphere and does not destroy the street scene; the use of a hill village in Italy as a holiday centre; and a new hotel in Yugoslavia that was once a group of ordinary buildings on a promontory connected to the mainland by a causeway. London has some good examples of warehouses that have been converted to provide restaurants.

Using existing buildings will require an imaginative approach on the part of the architect in order to exploit the whole of the interior spaces and the quality of original detail to the full. The external features of the building and its relationship with its surroundings must not, however, be ignored.

Extending an existing building is another possibility. In this case the plan should be carefully considered from both the internal and external points of view with the aim of producing a solution that has a natural flow to it and avoids compromises as far as possible. Externally the designer will be faced with the problem of whether to integrate or to contrast his design with the surroundings, but in either case the solution must be a compatible one. Good, honest buildings will, in most cases, give a good result, avoiding purely fashionable design cliches.

Very small extensions to an old building may need to be treated in the same way as the original in terms of construction and materials. Wherever possible, however, a modern design should be chosen as this will give the best functional results plus good appearance. The

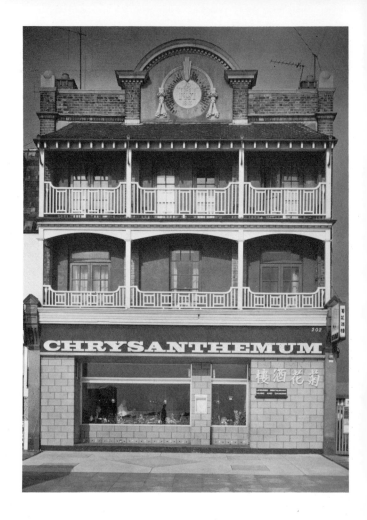

The quality of the original building has been skilfully exploited in this conversion
Opposite, a striking modern restaurant making use of old castle walls

34

contrast with the original building will enhance both of them.

Conservation areas are also a challenge to designers and owners. Conservation is not the same thing as preservation, and good, modern buildings, extensions and infilling will be much more acceptable than, say, mock Georgian buildings in a real Georgian conservation area. Quality is a difficult word to define in architectural terms, but the soundness of materials, the depth of modelling of surfaces, surface finishes, and proportion all play a part in achieving a satisfactory whole. It is important to consider the total building in this context.

There are many prefabricated buildings and systems on the market, from complete buildings and extensions to part units and components. Before deciding to use a prefabricated system a feasibility study should be carried out, analysing possible systems in detail and comparing them with alternative, traditional methods. A realistic evaluation of how appropriate this method will be can then be made.

In the case of complete buildings and extensions, the following points must be considered:

1 Cost of substructure
2 Cost of superstructure
3 Cost of services
4 Cost of furnishings and fittings
5 Speed of construction
6 Quality of finished building related to planning requirements and existing environment
7 Finishes and maintenance costs
8 Life expectancy
9 Soundproofing and insulation – lightweight materials used for floors and walls may not be very soundproof, weight is the best soundproofing ingredient in any material
10 Fire officer's requirements

There have been significant developments in the field of smaller prefabricated units, including complete bathroom units with services installed ready for plumbing in to the mains.

Advertising and signs

Hotels and restaurants need to attract the attention of casual visitors as well as those who have book a room or a meal, and both types of visitor will want to be able to find their way without frustration or fatigue.

The first step is to assess the approach: if it is obvious and straightforward relatively little signposting will be required, with perhaps only the name being shown. If the approach is from a high-speed road, signs must be of a sufficient size and positioned so that drivers have enough time to react safely without endangering other road users. In towns in particular, the impact of signs and the general quality of the surrounding neighbourhood must be taken into consideration.

In many cases signs will need the approval of the local authority planning department and they should therefore be consulted at an early date. This is particularly necessary in the case of conservation areas. Floodlit and illuminated signs require planning approval.

Once guests have been attracted to the building, further signs will be needed to direct them and external lighting will be needed at night. The general effect of both signs and lighting needs to be carefully considered, during the day as well as at night.

Floodlighting

In recent years, floodlighting has come to play an increasingly important part in attracting the attention of the public to buildings such as hotels and restaurants.

Floodlighting should not be dismissed as being over-expensive. Small spotlights and floodlights suitable for external use are relatively cheap to buy and are not particularly costly to run. The aim of any floodlighting scheme should be to enhance the building and its surrounding landscape, picking out particular features of interest and complementing the quality of the building as seen by daylight. This can often be done with a quite small installation. Too little thought is given to the impact of even a small amount of floodlighting of a single tree, a group of shrubs, a stretch of water, a fountain, or a part of the building.

Consultation with the local authority planning department will be necessary and their approval should be sought for any scheme.

4 INTERIOR DESIGN: hotels and motels

The design of the interior of a hotel or motel will have a large bearing on the comfort and satisfaction of guests using it. A well conceived plan carried out with care and attention to detail but avoiding gimmicks and over-fashionable features that will date rapidly should be the aim. Motels and hotels differ somewhat in their requirements, so in the discussion of the major elements of the interior that follows, motels are mentioned separately.

Reception areas
The reception area of a hotel sets the scene for guests and is the hub of their activities. It needs to be as large as possible and with some visual impact; the counter in particular provides an opportunity for good, imaginative design.

The natural flow of guests and visitors from taxis, public transport or car park should be towards the reception area. The effect to aim at should be one of welcome, with a confident, relaxed, but efficient atmosphere. A central reception position will help, particularly in small hotels where staffing can be a problem in slack periods. There should be ample space for baggage and for guests to congregate, both on arrival and on departure. Hotels that cater for large parties or groups will obviously need more space than those where guests arrive in small numbers at a time.

From the reception area there should be clear, well signed routes to other facilities within the hotel, with easy access to the staircase or lift to bedroom floors. The reception area is an important one from the point of view of security and the desk should be sited with this in mind.

Counter space in the reception area should be adequate to cope with peak demand and a decision must be made as to whether to have chairs or not. A counter for standing at generally provides more space for large numbers of people. The space available for a reception area will depend on the size of the building and the type of establishment. In a small hotel the receptionist will

Reception areas need to be imaginatively designed while remaining functional and attractive

KEY ELEMENTS OF RECEPTION AREAS

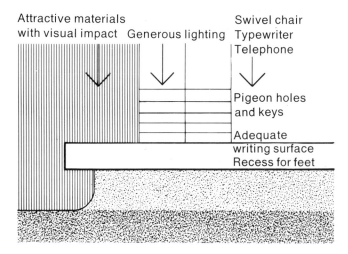

37

The type of reception will vary with the nature of the operation and its clientele

be responsible for several operations: receiving guests, making out bills, typing, telephones, issuing keys and so forth. The ergonomics of the desk space will therefore be critical and a minimum need for movement will speed up the process. Well designed key-boards with adjacent pigeon holes for messages will help. In large hotels a safe-deposit system will certainly be needed.

If possible, there should be a waiting area or lounge with seating close by the reception area. Its size will depend upon the space available and it may have to be sacrificed in a small hotel, in which case some seating should be provided in the reception area. The welcoming effect of a well designed lounge that can be seen from the reception desk should not be underestimated, and signs to the lounge and other facilities should make guests feel that these are readily available.

Motel receptions should be considered in the same way as those in hotels, but where cars are parked close to the bedroom accommodation the reception must be sited for easy access from parked cars. If the accommodation can be seen from the reception desk this will help to direct guests and it also provides a subtle method of control. Motels frequently work on the principle of payment in advance on arrival with cash transactions for other facilities when they are used. This system enables guests to leave at any time and makes strict control less necessary.

Lounges, bars and television rooms

Some fundamental decisions must be taken before designing rooms for these purposes:

1 Is a separate TV room needed? This will be less likely in more expensive hotels where sets can be permanently installed or rented in bedrooms

2 Should there be quiet rooms for writing or reading? Again, these are less important if facilities are provided in bedrooms

3 What sort of bar trade is expected? Will the hotel or motel become the local pub? It may be necessary to have two or three different types of bar

4 What should be the quality of the main hotel bar? Can it be associated with the restaurant so that drinks before the meal while looking at the menu will help trade?

5 Should there be a garden room with a drinks service?

6 Should there be a children's playroom?

7 Should there be an outdoor terrace with the use of a garden?

Hotels are labour intensive by nature and the plan should be designed so that several areas can be served and supervised with minimum staff at quiet periods. A central bar service is therefore essential and a central service core arrangement will help in economical running.

Careful design of lounge and bar areas is needed to provide spaces where small groups can feel comfortable when the building is under-occupied and, at the same time, can give a sense of seclusion when full. Carpeting, furnishings and furniture are all very important, together with the quality of natural and artificial lighting. All these are discussed in greater detail in Section 6.

ADVANTAGES OF CENTRAL SERVICE AREA

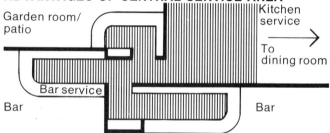

Garden room/patio

Kitchen service

To dining room →

Bar service

Bar

Bar

Bars and lounges need to be carefully designed if they are to be visually attractive, secluded when crowded and welcoming when empty

Patios and terraces

Rooms can be extended into the garden and the landscape by using patio and terrace areas. Reception areas, lounges, bars and restaurants can all be expanded in this way with advantage. Layouts should be planned to give adequate supervision and service. Bedrooms and studio rooms on the ground floor can have private terraces, giving a contrast with bedrooms on upper floors. If there is a good view this can be the focal point of outdoor spaces and the design of paving, screens, canopies and planting can play a lesser role. Small external spaces with no special visual qualities can be made more interesting by designing introspective schemes focusing on plants, water or sculpture.

The design of communicating doors and windows in rooms connecting with outdoor areas must be made as safe as possible by avoiding steps, sills, and large areas of glass that are difficult to see wherever possible. In use there should be the minimum obstruction. Some detailed points to consider are:

1 Shelter from wind
2 Protection from light rain or bright sun
3 Paving detail and material
4 Layout and design of furniture
5 The provision of umbrellas, sunshades or blinds
6 Plants and shrubs
7 The visual link with surrounding landscape
8 Design of surrounding walls
9 Lighting for use after dark
10 Special features such as fountains, plant containers and sculpture. Water features can be fairly inexpensive with the use of GRP and plastics liners and submersible pumps

Patios and terraces can be made more interesting by changes of level and variety in planting to provide a number of smaller, more intimate areas

Dining rooms and restaurants

This area is covered in detail in the next section, but there are some basic decisions to be made concerning its relationship with the rest of the hotel:

1 What level of catering will be appropriate?
2 Is lunchtime trade expected?
3 What competition exists in the area? Kitchens and restaurants are expensive in terms of space, equipment and staff, so they need to be fully utilised
4 Will breakfast be provided and, if so, will it be English or Continental? In motels a self-service breakfast in bedrooms may be more appropriate
5 Is there likely to be any conflict between the requirements of resident guests and casual visitors?
6 Will there be a demand for cheap, convenience foods throughout long periods during the day and evening?

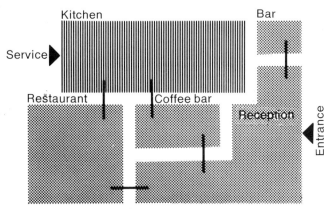

**COMMUNICATION BETWEEN ROOMS
FOR STAFF AND GUESTS**

Kitchens

Kitchens are covered in detail in the next section. The position of the kitchen will depend very much on the decisions taken about the type of restaurant to provide according to the headings given above. The kitchens must be strategically placed to give good service, adjacent to the dining room and with easy access for room service. A central position will mean that problems of noise and smells in main rooms and bedrooms will have to be overcome.

Dining rooms should be appropriate to the type of food provided and placed strategically in relation to other services

46

Bedrooms

Bedrooms come in all shapes and sizes, particularly if existing buildings are considered. There is less variety in new buildings and there is a growing trend towards the bedroom with bathroom en suite. The extra space required for this arrangement is fairly small and in fact an adequate small bathroom can be provided in an area 1·7m square. The cost of the extra plumbing is not very great if compared with the cost of providing a washbasin in the bedroom itself and the return from a higher room rate will be considerable. A central air conditioning system will probably not be necessary as inexpensive individual extractor units can be fitted to operate with the light switch and connected with a 150mm duct. A delay mechanism switches the fan off about 20 minutes after the light has been turned off.

Unless there is a big demand for single rooms which cannot be met by offering double rooms at reduced rates for single guests, single rooms may not be needed. There seems to be a trend towards shared rooms, which can take up very little more space than single rooms and will give greater flexibility to the hotel. Some typical arrangements are shown.

TYPICAL BEDROOM LAYOUTS

Bedroom suite with bathroom

3600 × 5600mm

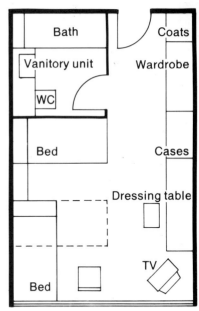

Luxury bedroom suite with bathroom

4000 × 6500mm

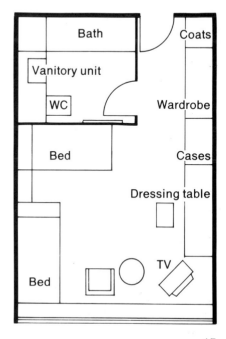

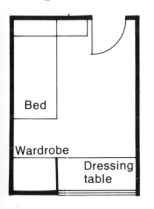

Single bedroom

2500 × 3300mm

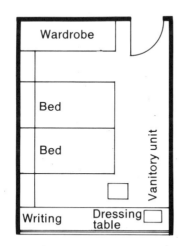

Double bedroom

3000 × 4200mm

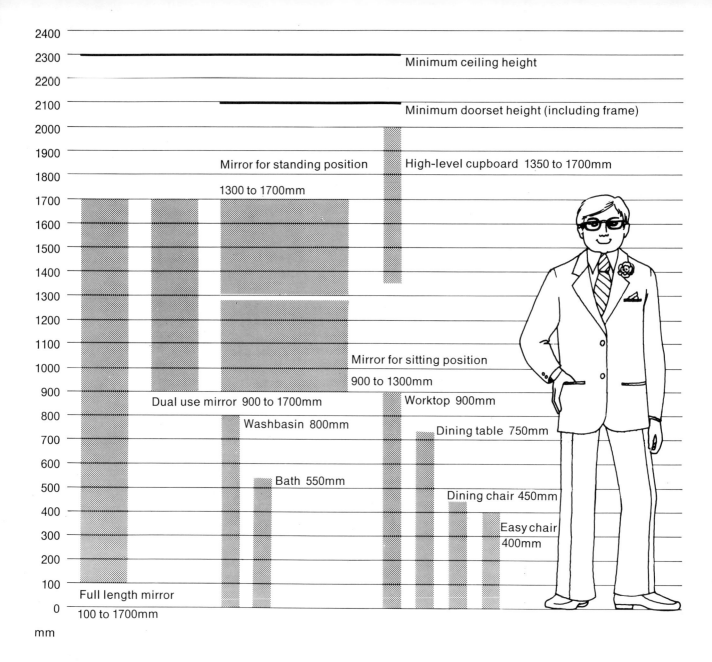

2400
2300 — Minimum ceiling height
2200
2100 — Minimum doorset height (including frame)
2000
1900
1800   Mirror for standing position   High-level cupboard 1350 to 1700mm
1700   1300 to 1700mm
1600
1500
1400
1300
1200
1100
1000   Mirror for sitting position
900   900 to 1300mm
800   Dual use mirror 900 to 1700mm   Worktop 900mm
700   Washbasin 800mm   Dining table 750mm
600
500   Bath 550mm   Dining chair 450mm
400   Easy chair
300   400mm
200
100   Full length mirror
0   100 to 1700mm

mm

IMPORTANT VERTICAL DIMENSIONS

This dining room makes the maximum use of an existing building, with
simple, complementary furnishings and decoration

Left and above, a bathroom and a bedroom both making extensive use of laminated plastics. Opposite, an imaginative use of colour for an outdoor seating area

51

Canopies can be used to define sitting areas and provide intermediate spaces between the interior and exterior of the building

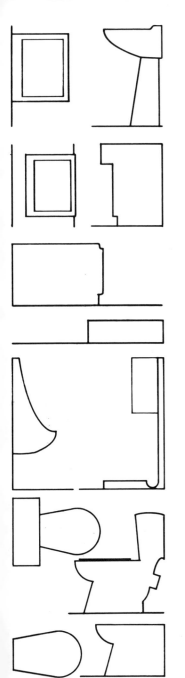

BATHROOM FITTING DIMENSIONS

Washbasins
Height 800mm average
Sizes 510×405mm
535×430mm
585×470mm
635×455mm

Vanitory units
Height 800mm
Depth from 500mm
Bowls 485×560mm
360×500mm
455×510mm

Baths
Height 550mm
Sizes 1675×725mm
1830×725mm
1675×710mm
1830×710mm
1675×675mm

Shower tray
Height 180mm
Sizes 610×610mm
720×760mm

Urinal
Floor to top 1065mm

Close coupled WC
Height 785mm
Projection 545mm
Width 370mm

Bidet
Height 405mm
Projection 545mm
Width 370mm

BATHROOM DIMENSIONS

Minimum shower/wash area right
1500×1500mm

Small bathroom below
1900×2000mm

Large bathroom below right
2100×2300mm

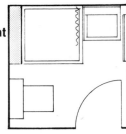

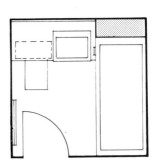

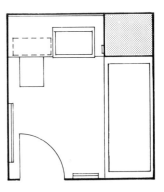

Conference rooms and exhibition areas

Facilities for conferences will widen the scope of the hotel and can double as banqueting rooms. The varying requirements of users will have to be considered and provision for acoustical and visual privacy will be needed if the room is to be subdivided for any purposes.

There must be adequate service areas, and, if the rooms are to be used for banqueting, they must be close to the kitchens and main service areas. There will need to be a reception and congregating area, with adequate toilet facilities. There is a growing demand for increasingly sophisticated audiovisual equipment.

A basic decision will be the amount of flexibility needed: it is less expensive to provide three separate spaces than a single large space with good sound-proof partitioning.

Adequate storage space for chairs and tables near the room is essential, and furniture should be carefully chosen. Chairs must be light and comfortable and should stack easily. Tables that can be linked together in different shapes are useful.

Ventilation needs careful consideration, particularly if the room is to be used for showing films or banqueting with large numbers of people. Care must be taken to ensure that the ventilation equipment is reasonably silent in use.

Space for trade displays or exhibitions associated with a conference will be useful near commercial centres. Adequate space, flexible lighting and adaptable display screens can be provided.

Additional facilities

Large hotels can offer a number of extra facilities, but the choice open to small establishments is more restricted. Sauna baths are comparatively small and inexpensive and are growing in popularity. An independent charge can be made for the use of these, and other, facilities. Swimming pools are expensive both in capital costs and running costs. In this country some form of heating is essential and will be a major expense.

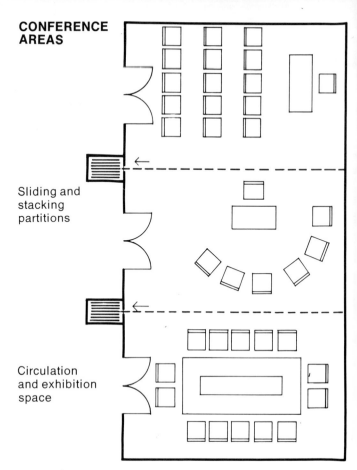

CONFERENCE AREAS

Sliding and stacking partitions

Circulation and exhibition space

Large conference area can be divided into three rooms for smaller meetings

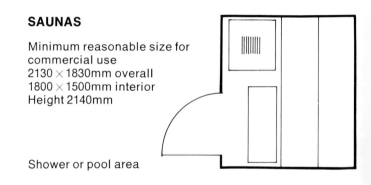

SAUNAS

Minimum reasonable size for commercial use
2130 × 1830mm overall
1800 × 1500mm interior
Height 2140mm

Shower or pool area

A major conversion can bring about a complete change of image

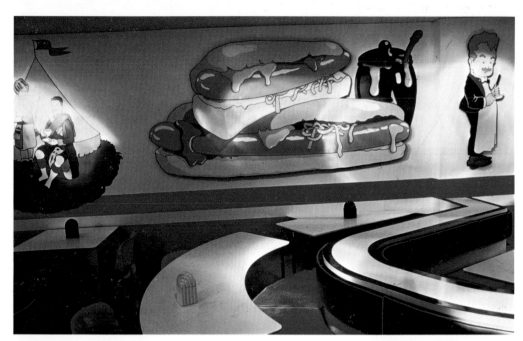

Snack bars and self-service restaurants often make use of bright colours and bold decoration to attract their clientele

5 INTERIOR DESIGN: restaurants and snack bars

The aim must be to provide an interior in which different types of guest can enjoy the food and the company to ensure that they remember the experience and return in the future. Each type of restaurant and snack bar will need a different treatment to satisfy the particular requirements of its clientele.

The space available will often be a challenge to the designer. Unconventional room shapes can be used to advantage to produce a homely, hospitable, congenial environment in which to eat, whereas a plain rectangular space may need more effort on the part of the designer to achieve the same sort of result.

Lighting in restaurants is of particular importance, and it can be used to transform the atmosphere after dark so as to make the surroundings for evening trade totally different from that during the day. The quality of the food itself is of equal importance and it must be geared to the type of establishment. A snack bar will build up a custom that is associated with convenience foods, although there are now many snack bars extending their facilities. The choice of the right type of menu will contribute to the restaurant's success and, generally speaking, the more expensive the menu, the better the food and the more critical will be the guests. It is often better to offer a limited menu with good fresh food that changes from time to time, rather than the familiar long menu of frozen food which tastes the same in every restaurant.

The section that follows has been broken down into the main types of eating place, which can be restaurants in their own right or parts of a hotel or motel. With larger establishments the hotel complex might include several different types of restaurant.

The space requirement can only be decided after detailed planning consideration. As a guide, about 1·2 to 2·0 square metres of dining space should be allowed per person. The kitchen and preparation area should be about half this, or between 0·5 and 1·0 square metres, with an ancillary and storage area of between one and a half and two times the kitchen area. Any reduction in the kitchen area tends to reduce efficiency and speed of service.

Kitchens can be planned around the sort of flow diagram shown below. More complex and detailed diagrams can be produced depending on the scale of the catering establishment.

BASIC KITCHEN ORGANISATION

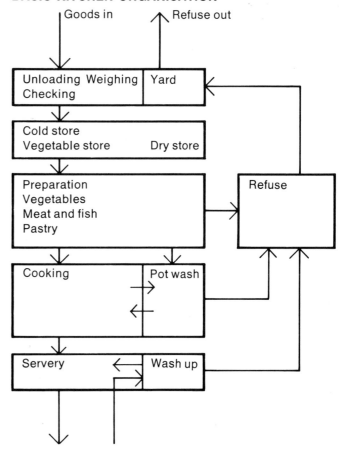

KITCHEN AREA FLOW DIAGRAM

A logical sequence of activities is important irrespective of size, from goods in to storage, preparation, cooking, servery and pot wash with strategically placed wash up. The office should be in a key position

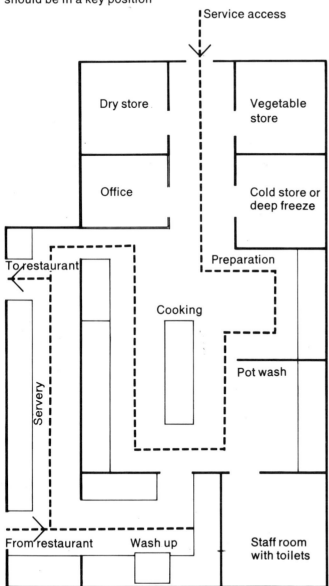

EATING AREAS

For two diners table size should be 700 × 600mm

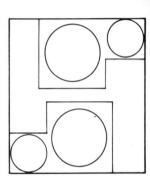

Dining table height 720mm
Clearance space beneath 600mm
Dining chair height 440 to 450mm

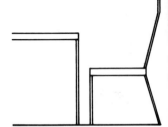

Fixed table and floor-mounted swivel chair
Table height 750mm
Chair height 450mm

Fixed stool at bar
Bar height 1050mm
Stool height 750mm
Footrest 250mm
Service side of bar height 900mm

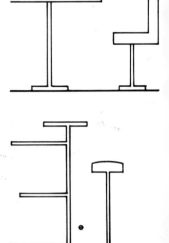

Previous page, a cool, restrained coffee shop to contrast with a busy store. Left, above and opposite, a highly atmospheric interior that makes great use of reflective surfaces, lighting and colour

Rectangular and square tables

Corridor space 900mm for service,
250mm for access

Minimum width of table
700mm

Minimum square table
for four 900 × 900mm

Four sitting opposite
at rectangular table
1200 × 750mm

Six with one at each
end at rectangular
table 1500 × 75mm

Six with three each
side 1800 × 750mm

Eight with one at each
end 2400 × 750mm

Eight with four each
side 2300 × 750mm

Circular tables

Minimum diameter
for one 750mm

For two 850mm

For four 1050mm

For six 1200mm

For eight 1500mm

Banquettes and tables

Width from back to back
will vary from
1650 to 1930mm

Any additional space
taken up between
backs of seats

Table width 600mm

Length 1140 to 1220mm

Corners rounded
for ease of access

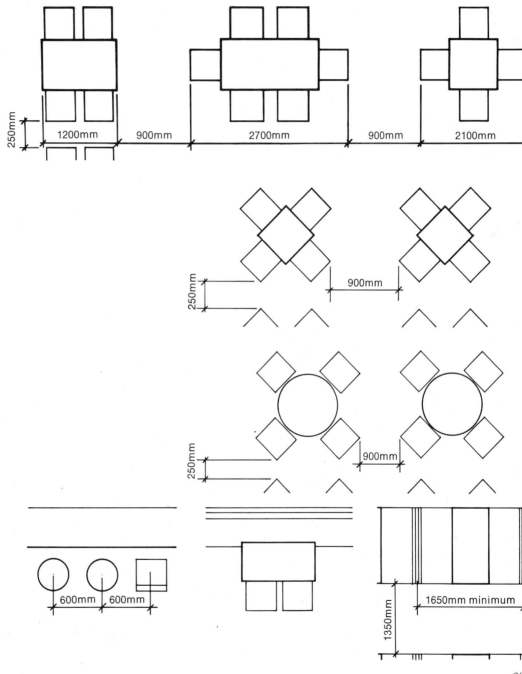

Snack bars, bistros, cafés and pubs

The optimum seating capacity for this type of eating place seems to be between 50 and 60 and the aim must be to have a rapid turnover of trade at the peak periods during lunchtime and in the evening. The interior design should generally be gay and fresh, clean rather than clinical, and appeal to people looking for a quick snack and in particular to the young. The seating should be comfortable initially, but not specially so for long periods: somewhat vertical seating will take up less space and allow the maximum number of seats in a given space. At the same time it will encourage customers to move on and make room for others. Good control will be essential to make the snack bar easy to run and the service counter, kitchen, washing up and service areas need to be carefully located.

The kitchen will handle mainly convenience foods and make use of griddles, microwave ovens and the like. These have the added attraction of letting the customers see what is being cooked and encouraging them to collect cold foods, sweets and drinks on their way to the pay counter, where their hot dishes will be ready and waiting. The main elements in the design will be:

1 A self-service counter where hot food can be ordered and cold foods, sandwiches, sweets and drinks can be collected
2 Dishwashing facilities with either a door from the main eating area for service staff or a return counter
3 The kitchen area, forming part of the counter with griddles, microwave ovens, hot drinks units, frying unit, warming cupboards and warmed serving counters with lamps and bains marie
4 A service area with space for empty goods, a cold room, refrigerators and an office
5 Employees' toilet and small rest room
6 Eating area
7 Customers' toilet

Some imagination is needed to create the right impression and the normal shop unit of width 5–6m and depth 12–15m will have to be used. An illusion of space is essential: mirrors can be used but too many of them may become monotonous and ineffective.

The high occupancy rate of a successful snack bar

The horizontal beams of the roof of this park restaurant provide visual interest while fully glazed walls give a good view out

Snack bars, cafés and pubs have high occupancy rates, and finishes must be chosen accordingly

means heavy wear on all materials and surfaces so a good design will have high wear resistance while not appearing too clinical. Some contrast in flooring materials, with carpets in sitting areas, can be successful for example. Fabrics for seating must be hard wearing and easily cleaned, as must be counter tops and tables. Wall surfaces, paints and wallpaper can need frequent replacement and more permanent surfaces of brick, timber, stone or plastics laminate may be more satisfactory, softened by the use of pictures and drapes. Ceilings are also important as they can be used to absorb sound, and hide services. Changes of level will emphasise different areas. There must be adequate air extraction over cooking areas to avoid damage to interior finishes. In all cases, the fire officer and building inspector must be consulted to avoid problems concerning fire resistance and the surface spread of flame.

The coffee shop is becoming an important part of many hotels and can contrast with more formal dining facilities

Self-service restaurants

Self-service restaurants have many features in common with snack bars. The kitchens are more extensive to provide a wider range of food and are often visible from the eating area, which promotes confidence among customers. The more elaborate kitchen in the self-service restaurant will need a careful study of work flow, from storage through preparation and cooking to the serving counter, avoiding the return circulation of dirty plates and cutlery to the washing area.

A careful study must be made of the number of people who are likely to use a self-service restaurant so that the counter area can be planned to avoid long queues. This will help the establishment to work efficiently and have a rapid turnover during peak periods. Self-service restaurants may be independent, part of a hotel, or connected with commercial or industrial premises. The main elements will be:

1 A self-service counter with space for collecting trays and passing along to pick up cold food from display shelves and hot food from griddle and frying units

2 A section for salads, sandwiches, cakes, cold sweets and drinks

3 The cashier, who should be strategically placed to help direct the flow of customers

4 The main seating area, which must be large enough to cope with peak demand

In large self-service restaurants it may be better to separate foods from drinks to avoid long queues of disgruntled customers who want a light snack or a quick drink but no cooked food.

The service area will comprise a large storage area, including refrigerators and cold stores, together with defrosting and warming-up apparatus, fish friers, microwave ovens, warm cupboards and bains marie.

The staff will require toilets, a rest room and possibly changing facilities. Customers will also require toilets.

The interior should be planned to give a free flow from the entrance past the self-service counter to the seating. Interior finishes will be similar to those discussed under snack bars, but care will have to be taken with larger premises to avoid an over clinical appearance. Efficient ventilation and extraction will be needed to prevent cooking smells from penetrating the eating area.

Restaurants

This is a general heading to cover all the many types of independent restaurants and those in hotels that are not described in other sections. A clear design brief will be necessary in the absence of any direct connection with a particular type of establishment. This will depend on the overall nature of the hotel, motel or restaurant, taking into account the grade, quality and service provided throughout the building and the special requirements of the clientele. The approach should be to produce a feasibility study and a brief covering all the points described in Section 1. Studying the type of menu to be provided will help the designer to solve the problems of arranging the kitchen, serving area and dining space. It may be worth incorporating a theme associated with the locality or the name of the restaurant. It can be an advantage to attract custom by encouraging people to say 'meet me at the Buffalo Restaurant' for example and have a western theme. A separate entrance can be provided to attract casual visitors and give the restaurant a separate identity from the hotel.

The brief will establish the level of service, the number of seats and overall staff requirement. Careful planning of the service area should include consideration of the pattern of circulation, the position of the head waiter and cashier. The size of establishment is important, as small restaurants will have to employ a single person to carry out a number of functions.

There are an infinite number of ways to arrange the layout and pattern of this type of restaurant. In all cases, the atmosphere created by an overall theme, together with the arrangement of seats and tables, will play a vital role in the success of the restaurant. The majority will prefer a table round the edge of the room where there is more privacy, alcoves and tall-backed chairs will help to do this in the centre of the room. However, this will not be universally acceptable and in some hotels a more traditional layout is more appropriate.

Changes of level create interest within the restaurant, but they also give rise to problems for staff and make trolley service very difficult.

Mood is a difficult thing to describe, depending as it does on many factors of lighting, colour and atmosphere. It plays an important part in the design and can

be changed in the same space effectively with the price structure of the menus at different times of the day. For example, if lunches are provided at low prices during the day, a high-priced menu in the evening will require an interior that can be transformed, perhaps by different lighting and a change in seating layout, to justify the difference in price. A change in the menu will not be found to be sufficient on its own.

High-class restaurants

For this type of restaurant the descriptions in the previous section apply, except that the degree of luxury will be greater, depending on the price of food and the need for more attention to both detail design and space allocation. Luxury restaurants have to condition guests to higher prices; the atmosphere must be right and there should be ample space for them not only to enjoy the meal but also to have a leisurely drink beforehand when choosing their food. The customers' needs for privacy must be taken into account and seclusion provided by using an alcove type of plan or by having enough space between tables to make it difficult to overhear conversation at other tables. The higher the price the greater will be the demands on the skill of the designer and the chef. Guests having a gourmet meal will be critical of shortcomings and so the detail design from the moment they arrive will be very important.

Restaurants serving good food at high prices should have interesting and high-quality interiors

Atmosphere contributes to the enjoyment of food and a regional flavour can be combined with a modern interior design

Specialised restaurants

A vast number of specialised restaurants exist throughout our towns and cities, and it is sad to find that very few of these take a constructive approach to design. Not enough thought is given to the possibilities of illusion in conditioning customers to the type of food to be provided. One's surroundings have an effect on appetite and food will be appreciated all the more if it is eaten in an interesting interior that reflects its country of origin. Eating a Chinese meal in a restaurant that previously served Indian food and has only had a few pictures changed fails miserably as an occasion.

One problem facing the designer is to establish requirements in detail, and the specialist restaurant provides a wonderful opportunity of introducing a natural theme for the interior. Study the traditional restaurants of the country of origin of the food and, with larger countries, the particular area the food comes from. Competition is all-important and so it makes economic sense to attract clientele by the surroundings as well as the menu. It is best to avoid looking at the westernised style of large hotels abroad. In Japan, for example, the typical modern hotel will offer very few ideas and it will be better to look at the traditional Japanese inn or eating house. Illusions can be created: it is not necessary for guests to sit on the floor or at very low tables to have an impression of a Japanese meal, but other parts of the atmosphere, such as cooking in front of the guests, could well be incorporated.

6 INTERIOR DESIGN: general aspects

Atmosphere

The atmosphere and mood produced by the interior design of a hotel or restaurant will affect the physical comfort and psychological attitude of guests. A successful design is a very important factor in producing an appreciative response.

The sort of feeling that should be aimed at will vary and is difficult to describe, but it is essential to try and get the right kind of reaction from the customer. One of the basic choices concerns the formality or informality of the design.

Formality is achieved by a regular layout of tables, a generally sophisticated design and a generous allocation of space. Informality, on the other hand, can be produced by dividing the space into small personal areas so as to give more individual privacy.

Choosing one or the other of these alternatives will start to set the scene. The next thing that the guest will be aware of will be the detail design of chairs, furnishings and fittings, and of the quality of small items such as table cloths. The cleanliness of the surroundings and the appearance of staff will also play a part.

All these, and other factors, will together produce the building's total mood. When making decisions it is important to consider the effect that changes in any of these factors will have on the rest. Themes can help a designer to create an atmosphere but a successful interior design will have to involve more than just decoration. The mood of guests will be spoilt if the menu, graphic design and the appearance and behaviour of staff do not contribute to the overall effect. Every item down to the smallest detail will have an effect on the atmosphere.

The aim must be to make a good first impression on the guests when they arrive and then to maintain this over a long period. This can only be achieved by good design: it is not enough to create an impression of a certain type of interior if guests then find, on later inspection, that it is all an illusion with, for example,

'Tudor' beams made of plastic within touching distance. The subtle difference between imitations and the genuine article will almost certainly be noticed by the discerning guests and frequently modern copies are by no means a cheap substitute for the real thing. A good designer will exploit the characteristics of materials without trying to produce a sham effect.

Eating areas should seem relaxed and comfortable, with surroundings that are in tune with the food. Reception areas should give an impression of being friendly and welcoming as well as being efficient. Lounges must be pleasant to sit in and good places to meet friends. Restaurants must achieve an atmosphere that provides guests with pleasant memories of the food and their surroundings. Circulation spaces must be laid out in a way that helps the visitor to forget the distances between different facilities; in large hotels this becomes more difficult as corridors increase in length. The atmosphere in corridors is often overlooked and a welcome break in the row of doors with, perhaps, a glimpse of the garden or a well designed display of lighting, a painting or some other work of art will help to break up the distance. The same sort of thing can be done in lounges or dining spaces. The colour, furnishings, layout and facilities provided in bedrooms will also affect the senses of the customer.

In the case of conversions and alterations it is important to make a detailed study of what already exists so that the potential, not only of the space, but also of the materials, features and fittings already present can be exploited. The imaginative designer will accept the challenge and produce an interior with a distinctive character.

Colour and materials

Colour is like lighting in that it can have the maximum effect – for good or bad – at a minimum capital cost. Colour is a personal matter, but rather too much emphasis has been placed on this in the past and a good colour scheme will probably be recognised and admired irrespective of one's colour preferences.

Try to produce interesting colour schemes that will have a lasting effect and avoid too many fashionable colours in one area. This is not to say that fashionable colours should not be used; they can have great impact,

particularly in circulation and traffic areas where more vibrant colour and large-scale patterns can be used. But colours go out of fashion quickly and it is therefore better to use them in areas that are likely to be redecorated frequently.

The colour scheme should follow through the whole of the building, but careful consideration should be given to each separate area to create the right atmosphere. In lounges and bedrooms, for example, restful colours should be used, whereas in circulation areas one can be more bold and in eating areas exciting and stimulating surroundings are essential.

Among points to consider are that darker floor colours produce a good base and generally show fewer marks, although black itself will show all white spots and dust. Natural colours, whether light or dark, generally wear well. Dark painted windows, particularly glazing bars, will give the impression of being larger than they really are, so light colours are preferable here. Windows and doors have the further problem of opening and exposing otherwise hidden surfaces and colour clashes can occur at this point. The change of colours from one room to another and the need to link spaces with carpet colours, or the colours of skirtings, doors, or ceilings, should be considered. Dark colours tend to show up surface imperfections more than light colours.

The colour of bar tops and tables can affect the appearance of many drinks. Beers and red wines are good seen against browns and reds while yellow, green and blue detract.

It is essential to study the existing surfaces carefully in order to choose appropriate materials for coverings or paint colours, so as to emphasise or subdue the quality of the space and the surfaces. Colours fade and materials wear and clients will be conscious of a run-down establishment. It is advisable to have a chart for maintenance, repainting and refurbishing, so as to have a balanced expenditure over a period of some years.

Floor coverings

When it comes to choosing materials for floors, walls and ceilings, it is helpful to divide the materials into groups to begin with. Flooring can be classified into three main groups: hard floor finishes, medium floor finishes and soft floor finishes. The hard finishes have the great advantage of giving maximum wear resistance and they require little attention other than cleaning and occasional polishing. They are, on the other hand, noisy and dust tends to accumulate on them and is then transferred onto nearby carpets. Rugs can be added to give a feeling of greater warmth, but care will be needed to avoid hazards of tripping and slipping. Natural hard floor materials are often of very high quality and contrast well with soft floor finishes. Where heavy traffic is expected they can withstand wear better than any other type of surface.

Medium floors, including thermoplastic, vinyl, lino, rubber and cork finishes, are medium both in density and wearing quality. Thin surface coverings tend to reflect the quality of the base on which they are laid and if light shines on them at an angle it will show up any imperfections. The quality of these finishes does not come up to that of the hard surfaces and can, in many cases, have a rather domestic look. Before using them, therefore, pay very careful attention to the overall quality aimed at in the interior of the completed building.

Soft floor finishes are covered in greater detail in the section on furnishings. They include a very wide range of types and qualities.

Wall coverings

Walls can be covered in many different materials, but the fire officer must always be consulted in the case of public buildings and one's choice will be restricted in many areas depending on the classification of spread of flame and fire resistance. Colour can be provided simply by using paint in emulsion, eggshell, or gloss form. The greater the degree of sheen the more imperfections will show and if a poor surface is to be treated it will be best to choose a textured paper instead or apply paint over wood-chip paper.

Walls can be covered with paper, vinyl wall coverings, silk, wool, Japanese grass-cloth, reflective papers, and so on. Again, the amount of imperfections in the surface must be taken into consideration as surfaces with defects will show through to some extent, particularly with glossy surface finishes. Silks and other textiles were traditionally stretched on battens fixed to walls. There is now a French system that can be used to fix fabrics and leathercloth to walls.

Panelling in the form of wood or plywood boards, prefinished or with other decorative surfaces, can also be used. This sort of treatment has been restricted in some areas as the result of changes in the Building Regulations.

Tiles of ceramics or metal, or other natural materials such as brick, marble and stone, can also be considered, together with the vast range of plastics laminates and corks. Wall surfaces, like floors, will have a very great effect on the quality of the finished buildings, both in a visual sense and in terms of wear resistance. Fashion can be a problem, particularly when moving away from wallpapers, which have a limited life, towards plastics laminates in which the patterns may look reasonable when chosen but not four or five years later when ideas about colour and pattern have changed. It may be necessary to replace materials, not because they are worn out, but because their appearance is no longer satisfactory, so that a high initial capital cost does not necessarily result in a long-term saving on maintenance.

Ceiling coverings

The types of material that can be used for ceiling coverings are infinite, but choice is restricted by two major considerations: fire resistance, including the Building Regulations requirements for spread of flame; and acoustic properties.

Materials to be considered include plaster, fibrous plaster which can be moulded, timber in the form of hard or soft wood boards, panelling or sheets, and so on. Acoustic tiles can be obtained in a vast range of patterns and materials, some of which will satisfy quite stringent fire regulations, but these tend to be rather expensive.

When considering an existing building and the treatment of its floors, walls and ceilings, consider the general character of the buildings in order to exploit the potential of existing surfaces, materials and shapes. The following list is intended to stimulate ideas for finishes in different parts of the building, but it is obviously not exhaustive: it might be a good idea to have carpet on the ceiling in some areas – unlikely, but it can't be ruled out. Carpet does, of course, make a good wall-covering where extreme wear is expected.

Lighting

Lighting is one of the most important considerations in the design of buildings generally, and hotels and restaurants in particular require even greater attention in this respect. Lighting has a fundamental effect on the quality of an interior at very modest capital cost.

First and foremost, plan the interior taking both natural and artificial lighting into account, and produce a general description of the different visual effects required in different parts of the building. Good lighting can transform a dull interior into an exciting place and radically alter its mood from day to night. Lighting should emphasise the features of the plan.

Natural light coming from outside the building will be affected by the type and design of windows, and their position relative to walls and ceilings. It will be necessary to consider, in addition to the internal lighting effect, the external view and the space beyond the interior, bearing in mind the transformation that will occur at night when curtains are drawn or outside areas are floodlit. Lighting gives the designer a wonderful opportunity of emphasising the contrast between night and day.

For artificial lighting, functional requirements are fully covered in the code of the Illuminating Engineering Society. The IES suggest the following levels:

Restaurants 50–100 lux
Lounges and bars 100 lux
Halls and stairs 200 lux
Reception and serving 400 lux

These figures are only for guidance and are not mandatory. They do, however provide a starting point from which to assess the special requirements of a particular building.

Atmosphere can be created by differences in lighting levels, with subtle variations between areas for relaxation and work areas such as kitchens. The colour scheme for the interior will play an important part in determining the amount of light required: a dark interior with few reflecting surfaces will need more general light than one finished in light tones. Some variation is essential and the skill of the designer will be apparent in the finished scheme. When changing the level of lighting in different parts of a room, it is a good thing to be aware of the various effects that different types of light fitting

Reception and bars

Concentrated light on important features helps to direct guests and adds interest to displays

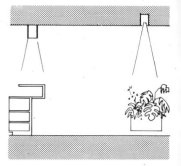

Lounge

Different levels of light are needed for reading and relaxing and to provide interest. Curtains can be lit by concealed fluorescent strips or wall washers

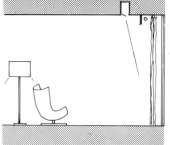

Restaurant

Individual lighting for each table is effective. It can be in the form of table lights, down lights or candles

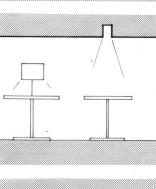

Bedroom

Good lighting is needed over mirrors and for reading in bed

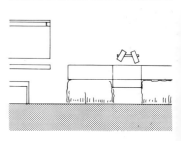

*Top and far right, downlighters
are good, unobtrusive light sources.
Bottom, spotlights and floodlights*

can produce. Down-lighters set flush with the ceiling, for example, produce a dramatic effect by leaving the interior reasonably dark but concentrating light directly below them. The glass and silver on a dining table will take on another dimension if lit in this way. Very sudden changes of level of illumination, however, should be avoided. The momentary blindness experienced on entering a room having been in bright sunlight will apply equally in very brightly lit and dark rooms. Working areas such as kitchens, offices, the reception area and the cash point will all require efficient lighting. Where additional lighting is needed within areas of subdued lighting, this can be provided by concentrating light close to the area of operation. Extremes of contrast can spoil the interior, however, and so considerable care must be taken to avoid a very bright light source at the actual point of contact with the desk. Service areas must also have less light at the point of transition with other rooms so that, for example, the brightly lit interior of the kitchen does not flood the dining room with light each time the door is opened when a meal is being served.

There are some general points to be considered when choosing light fittings. The first is to decide on the right type of lighting for the purpose: direct, indirect, static or adjustable in intensity. Tungsten fittings are more expensive to run than fluorescent ones, but they are generally more flexible in use and give a softer type of light. On the other hand, fluorescent lighting is cheaper to run and it can be used not only in work areas but also anywhere that the light source itself will not be seen – for example for pelmet lighting, where the indirect light provided will not contrast too sharply with tungsten fittings in the area.

Heat build-up from light fittings can be a source of serious embarrassment: tungsten fittings generate a considerable amount of heat, particularly if they are grouped together, and spotlights intensify the heat on the lighted area. Heat recovery systems are available linking the fitting and air conditioning plant, but these are not likely to be of much use in smaller buildings. An interior space with no windows where lighting is used throughout the day may need more ventilation and less heating due to the heat from the light fittings.

Downlighters

Spillring fitting gives a medium width beam with a very soft edge and is an ideal low brightness source

Pinhole fitting gives a wide-angle beam with minimum source brightness

Multigroove fitting gives dramatic display lighting to concentrate light on tables

Spotlights

A wide range of spotlight fittings are available using internal reflector spot and flood lamps

Wall washers should be placed 1.0m from the wall and about 1.5m apart to give directional light on curtains and pictures

Silver parabolic reflector using a 100W crown silvered bulb appears dark when lit and is a good decorative display fitting As an alternative, a soft 22° lamp will give about half the level of illumination

Internal reflector lamps

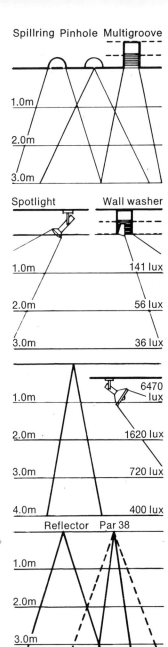

Reflector		Par 38	
100W 35°	150W 35°	100W Spot 15°	150W Flood 40°
900	2000	3750	2650 lux
230	500	940	660 lux
100	220	420	300 lux
55	125	230	170 lux

Light reflecting from the fitting itself, or from the surface on which the light falls, creates discomfort from glare and should be avoided where possible.

Light fittings are subject to changing fashion and can date the interior of a building. It is very difficult to avoid using some visible fittings, but a more lasting effect will be achieved by using a minimum of fashionable light fittings with the emphasis on concealed light sources. Carefully used, light can intensify the form and texture of spaces, surfaces and fabrics. It can also highlight objects of particular interest, works of art, plants and so on. It can even create illusions to change the shape and proportion of spaces.

Light fittings are designed for a given maximum wattage of bulb, and this is for the fitting used in normal conditions. Hotels frequently produce conditions that are abnormal as a result of unventilated spaces and the extra heat produced can be considerable. It is preferable, where possible, to choose fittings that are slightly larger than those stated by the manufacturer so as to enable a relatively smaller lamp to be used and so avoid the build-up of heat. The length of the bulb's life can be affected by overheating and the fittings themselves can be distorted.

Switching of lights needs careful consideration, not only in terms of functional requirements but also as a means of ensuring control, security and safety. The main methods are:

1 One-way, two-way and multiple switching
2 Master switching, except at mains and consumer units
3 Dimmer switches
4 Door-operated switches
5 Photo-electric cell switches to switch on lighting when a change of level of lighting occurs. This can be useful externally for floodlighting an entrance, for example
6 Switching can also be controlled by clocks, which can be manual, electric or solar operated. The last type have a mechanism to change switching-on times at different times of the year

In addition to the decorative effect created by lighting, there are certain statutory conditions of safety, such as exit signs, that must be considered.

Furnishings

Furnishings are a vital part of the interior of the building and cannot be considered in isolation. The interior, its decorative themes, and furnishings will all form part of the appraisal at this stage.

There are three essential criteria necessary for the proper selection of furnishings: function, aesthetic quality, and maintenance.

1 Function includes suitability for purpose, flexibility in use etc, relevant to the application
2 Aesthetic quality must be such that the furnishings fit into the visual concept of the building and also look good in isolation if seen on their own or are moved from one part of the building to another
3 Maintenance means that the furnishings must look good over a long period of time and be reasonably easy to keep clean

CARPETS AND SOFT FLOOR COVERINGS

The choice of carpets is extensive and it can be difficult to pick the right one. Wool with 20 per cent nylon to add strength is good; cotton, jute and sisal are less expensive but also less resistant to wear and fire spread. Other points to consider when choosing a carpet are:

1 Its quality related to anticipated wear and special circumstances of use
2 Expected traffic, especially if certain parts of the building will be subject to lots of people moving about. Main traffic areas across rooms may produce problems of greater wear
3 Visual appearance, in terms of colour and pattern
4 Cost. It is not always possible to assess value for money solely in terms of price. An expensive carpet may last longer and be an overall saving
5 Pile type, whether long, short, twisted, tufted, uncut or corded
6 Fire resistance. Carpets are vulnerable to cigarette burns, sparks from fires and so on. Nylon carpets tend to melt while wool carpets are self-extinguishing. Acrylics and viscose burn
7 Acoustics, since a sound-absorbing coefficient can be obtained for carpets. Carpets with a cut pile tend to absorb more sound than those with uncut pile. With cut pile, absorbtion increases as pile height and weight increase; with uncut pile, pile height is more important than pile weight. The type of fibre has little effect on acoustic performance. Any underlay greatly improves performance, and felt absorbs more noise than foam. Impact sounds are reduced in the following order: wilton or dense and short nylon pile carpet with felt underlay produce the best results for low, medium and high frequency sounds; tufted and fine gauge nylon with integral foam backing give medium results; and fibre bonded nylon surfaces and vinyl give fair and poor results respectively
8 Electricity. Problems can arise through carpets developing a static electrical charge. The shock that people walking on them receive depends on three factors: relative humidity, type of pile fibre, and construction of shoes. Static may be reduced or eliminated temporarily by applying an anti-static agent to the carpet, increasing the humidity, or by introducing a small proportion of conductive fibres into the carpet when it is made. Man-made fibre carpets develop more static than natural fibre ones
9 Durability. This can be a difficult matter. Nylon, for example, is resistant to wear although wool may retain its appearance over a longer period

In summary, it is hard to give general advice, but it does appear that the better the quality, the better the wear characteristics, and this could reduce capital costs over a long period. In areas with heavy traffic cheap floor coverings will not be satisfactory and it may be better to opt for another type of floor surface if money is short. Both long and short-term appearance will have to be taken into consideration, but it is difficult to be specific here as maintenance costs may be as much as 50 per cent less than with some hard floor finishes. The use of carpet can also help to reduce fuel costs and expenditure on other acoustic materials.

Rugs can be used both as floor coverings and as hangings and there is a vast range to choose from. The considerations mentioned under carpets apply equally to rugs, with the further point that safety must be considered. Slipping rugs and loose edges must be avoided.

CURTAINS, DRAPES AND NETS

Curtains can do more than just close off windows at night; they can give a new dimension to rooms and create the illusion of large or small windows, for example by covering walls completely. There are three main lengths of curtain to be considered:

1 Floor to ceiling, which gives a very generous effect to the window
2 From top of window to floor
3 From top of window to window-sill

Curtaining materials for use in hotels and restaurants will have to withstand the rigours of regular cleaning as dirt, grime and grease can be a big problem. Good quality materials are likely to stand up to this treatment much better than cheaper ones, but care must be taken to avoid very delicate materials that need special cleaning treatments. Remember that curtains may need lining to keep out light; special lining is needed for heat insulation and reflecting sunlight, in the case of large windows. Fire is a constant hazard in hotels and restaurants and most fabrics can be fire-proofed at little extra cost.

In terms of colour and pattern, the overall colour scheme for the interior must be taken into account as the richness and brilliance of the interior will depend very much on the choice of curtain material. Some colours fade and if the windows are exposed to long periods of sunlight it is worth checking with manufacturers in advance.

As far as size is concerned, floor to ceiling curtains should reach to within about two centimetres of the floor. In the case of curtains to a window-sill the length depends on the position in which they are hung: if they are on the outside of the window they should come about five centimetres below the sill; if to the window board this should be reduced to about two centimetres to minimise problems of dust and dirt. The width of curtains depends on the type of heading and fabric used. Generally speaking it is preferable to have additional fullness of material even with a cheap fabric. As a guide, the following should help:

Gathered – $1\frac{1}{2}$ times track length
Gathered nets – 2 times track length
Pencil pleats – 2 times track length
Pencil pleated nets – 3 times track length
Pinch pleats – 2 times track length
Pinch pleated nets – $2\frac{1}{2}$ to 3 times track length

The appearance of the curtains will be greatly affected

Gathered headings with standard tape are the simplest form of heading

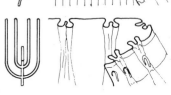

Pencil pleats with Regis tape give good appearance and are useful for most types of curtain

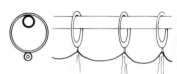

Pinch pleats need more skill and are used mainly for heavy fabrics and floor to ceiling curtains

Looped headings are decorative when used with timber or metal rails with matching rings

by the headings. The main types are illustrated here.

Net curtains are not simply a Victorian invention to obscure the view. A beautiful range of decorative nets and sun filters have been produced and can be used not only to improve the appearance of windows where there is an unattractive view, but also to change the quality of light coming through a window. Care must be taken when choosing the colour and pattern of nets as this will affect the amount of light they transmit. The other notes on curtains apply equally to nets.

Insufficient use is made of drapes in many interiors. Their softening effect on a room and the way in which they can transform a shape by, for example, curving a drape round two walls, can transform an unpleasant area into an attractive one. A door or window in a difficult position that affects the layout of furniture and upsets seating arrangements can be modified by using drapes to change the atmosphere in a way that would not be possible by other means.

Drapes, curtains and nets can be fixed to a wide variety of tracks. The basic choice is between visible and invisible systems.

Roller blinds can be made in a wide range of fabrics. Pinoleum or slatted wood blinds look good with foliage and plants

Pleatex blinds, made from tough paper, come in various colours and are cheap, but have a shorter life than wood, metal or plastics

Venetian blinds are made in metal, plastics or wood. Vertical blinds can be canvas, wood or man-made fabric

Shutters and screens are usually of timber, either solid or slotted, but may be fabric covered

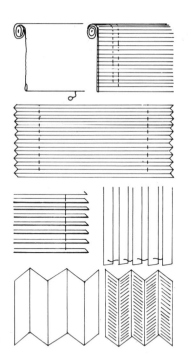

BLINDS

Many different types of blind are available. The main types are as follows:

1 Roller blinds are available in a wide range of materials, from curtain fabrics to waterproof blinds for bathrooms. In between these there are many washable and spongeable fabrics. It is better to choose a closely woven fabric that lies flat. The choice of colours is infinite

2 Pinoleums, slatted wood and quill blinds are also useful, particularly for garden rooms, terraces and so on, although they can, of course, be used elsewhere. They are made of very fine strips of wood, woven together with cotton, in either natural or stained colours. Heavier wooden slats can be effective in large areas

3 Balastores are made of specially strong pleated paper

4 Pleatex blinds are made of a wet-stretch kraft paper in plain colours. They are cheaper but less wear-resistant than other types

5 Venetian blinds can be of metal, plastics or wood. Care must be taken to remember the problems of dirt accumulating on horizontal surfaces and of noise when windows are open

6 Vertical louvre blinds can be made of man-made fabrics, wood slats, silk or canvas. Wooden blinds are expensive, but they do give a very warm effect in an interior

The choice of blinds depends to a large extent on the money available and the effect required. The majority of modern blinds are easy to operate.

SHUTTERS AND SCREENS

Unusual effects can be produced by using shutters and screens, both internally and externally. One can find examples of all sorts of shutters and screens for decorative and functional use by looking at old buildings in this country and buildings of any age on the continent.

LINEN, BEDCOVERS AND TOWELS

Looking at other fabrics for use in hotels in particular, the bed cover forms a very important part of the decorative scheme of the bedroom and so care must be taken in choosing the right fabric. The choice should be one that resists creasing and complements other fabrics and upholstery in the room. In the case of a studio room a cover can be made for pillows in the same fabric for use as a cushion.

When choosing sheets and blankets, take into account not only the capital cost but also long-term maintenance, ease of replacement and the comfort of guests. Some materials are less satisfactory in use than others and feel unpleasant to the touch. Cotton or a blend of cotton and man-made fibres are better in this respect than unblended man-made fibres. Blankets should be thick and fluffy. Wool is the traditional material, but it can be blended with man-made fibre. Colours and patterns must be considered in the light of long-term maintenance and the decorative scheme of the room. The same applies to duvets.

The same criteria apply to towels as to other linen. It is difficult to get away from the traditional white, but coloured towels can lend interest in a bathroom and this is an important factor. Cotton towels have the great advantage of being hardwearing, have excellent drying properties and feel soft and luxurious.

Furniture

The choice in furniture is between two main types: built-in and free-standing. Free-standing furniture can be chosen and bought from manufacturers' ranges. Commissioning designs for individual pieces of furniture can be expensive but it may be essential in order to get exactly the right effect for a particular room. In this case it is better to obtain a prototype before the real thing is produced in order to avoid some of the problems that can occur between the drawing board and production. The prototype should be well tested to make sure that its appearance is right and that no adjustments are needed before the order is placed.

As far as built-in furniture is concerned, the choice is between selecting from the growing range of kits available from manufacturers and purpose-built furniture. Mass-produced built-in furniture has considerable advantages because of the research that manufacturers carry out on its strength, stability, fittings and finishes. A very professional appearance at competitive prices can be obtained by selecting the right system. The following factors should be taken into account:

1 Proportion. Good design and visually satisfying proportions must be combined with stability, comfort and quality of finish
2 Materials must be suitable and in colours to fit the room scheme
3 Construction must be adequate to meet anticipated wear and tear
4 Maintenance. Has the manufacturer given enough thought to the cleaning, repair and general maintenance of the furniture?
5 Size. The scale of furniture is a difficult point on which to lay down rules. The problem is one of balancing the needs of the human scale with the spaces can get overcrowded. Avoid conflict between luxury areas will need generous furniture and small spaces can get overcrowded. Avoid conflict between tall and low furniture in a single area; most modern furniture tends to be low, whereas antique pieces are high. Consider the needs of the clientele: elderly people can find low chairs very difficult
6 Function. Consider the practical requirements the furniture will be expected to fulfil

7 Upholstery. The Design Council has put forward the following criteria for choosing upholstery: adequate strength; resistance to abrasive wear; resistance to burning; resistance to slipping of the component yarns; dimensional stability of the component yarns; colour fastness in light, rubbing and cleaning. These characteristics must be kept in mind when choosing upholstery as well as the appearance required. Fire-resistance and resistance to cleaning are particularly important in hotels and restaurants

There are two basic methods of upholstery: sprung and foam. It is also possible to have a combination of both these methods. It is important to choose the right construction for its purpose: furniture with deep buttoned velvet covered seating in a canteen would be as incongruous as wooden benches would be in an expensive restaurant.

Furniture for specific areas

The type of furniture chosen must be related to the area in which it is used. The illustrations and notes that follow are to stimulate ideas for furniture for specific purposes and to highlight some main considerations.

For reception areas and lounges, quality and comfort will make a big impact on guests. Grouping furniture round focal points can break down the scale of a large space. The balance between price and comfort is a delicate one. Bear in mind that old people find low furniture difficult to use.

For dining, restaurant and banqueting rooms, tables should be chosen for their flexibility in use, whether they can be stacked and linked, their cost, their resistance to damage and surface finish. It will be necessary to decide on the basic type of support: legs may be a problem and a central column can provide greater freedom of movement and possibly closer positioning of tables in the room. On the other hand, central supports are less stable, unless they are bolted to the floor. For chairs, the quality, cost, mobility, stacking ability and upholstery must all be taken into account. There is often some clash between the requirements of dining, with the emphasis on luxury, and the need to move chairs about, as in the case of banqueting rooms, where stacking chairs are essential. The diagrams that follow will help to assess the space required.

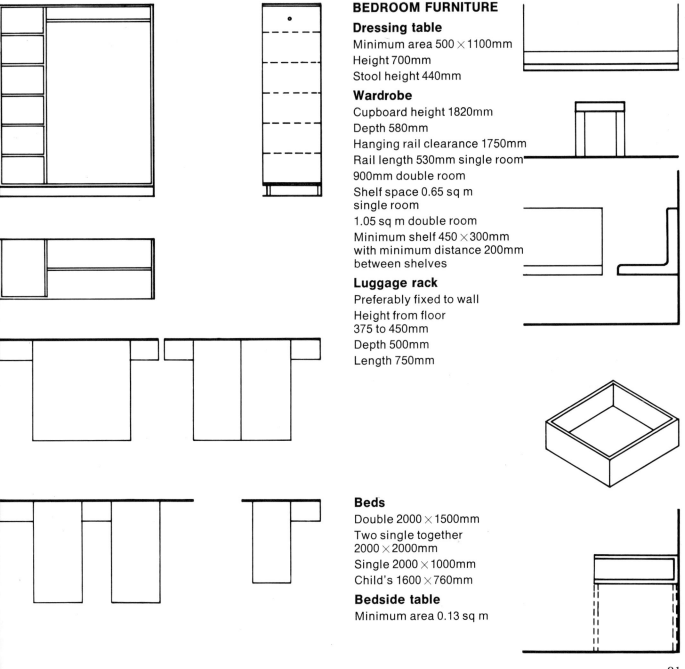

BEDROOM FURNITURE

Dressing table
Minimum area 500 × 1100mm
Height 700mm
Stool height 440mm

Wardrobe
Cupboard height 1820mm
Depth 580mm
Hanging rail clearance 1750mm
Rail length 530mm single room
900mm double room
Shelf space 0.65 sq m
single room
1.05 sq m double room
Minimum shelf 450 × 300mm
with minimum distance 200mm
between shelves

Luggage rack
Preferably fixed to wall
Height from floor
375 to 450mm
Depth 500mm
Length 750mm

Beds
Double 2000 × 1500mm
Two single together
2000 × 2000mm
Single 2000 × 1000mm
Child's 1600 × 760mm

Bedside table
Minimum area 0.13 sq m

Dumb waiters at service points need careful specification. In addition to storage for cutlery, china, sauces and condiments, it may be necessary to have refrigerated storage. Equipment is available or it can be purpose-built to fit in with an interior design.

At bars, fixed stools or moveable ones should be chosen to fit in with the surrounding materials. Snack bar banquet seating is frequently used and fixed with a central column bolted to the floor carrying a swivel-top, self-centering stool. For free-standing tables and chairs stability will be an important consideration. Flexible table systems with interchangeable tops can be used.

Bedroom furniture will comprise beds, cupboards, side tables, dressing tables, case racks and some occasional furniture.

Furniture for exterior use must be chosen according to whether it will be kept outside permanently or brought in during bad weather and at night. Resistance to sun and rain are important.

Folding tables and chairs are useful for emergency use since they are relatively cheap and take up less space than conventional stacking designs. They must, however, be carefully chosen to avoid down-grading the establishment.

Antique furniture can range from the inexpensive to practically priceless. It can make a wonderful contrast to modern furniture in the right setting. Beautiful old buildings need particular care: reproduction and mock antique furniture can look phoney and therefore make even original pieces in the room seem suspect. It is usually better to contrast simple modern designs in good materials with beautiful old pieces rather than trying to copy them. But avoid the modern cliche design and remember that today's antique was once a modern piece. Good pieces of any period will probably go together.

Cafeteria and snack-bar seating can be made of timber or steel; steel being stronger but more expensive. Expanded PVC is a good upholstery material and easy to clean. A seat foam of three to four inches will give good comfort. Seat height should be about 450mm as this will make the most use of the floor space and ensure a fairly upright posture, which will deter clients from lingering too long.

GENERAL FURNITURE

Easy chairs
Small chair without
arms 700 × 750mm
Chair with arms 850 × 850mm

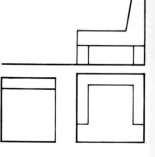

Upright chair 400 × 450mm
Occasional table
Stool 350 × 350mm

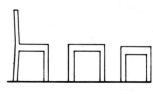

Upright piano
1520 × 660 × 1300mm
high

Grand piano 1520 × 1380
to 2740 × 990mm high

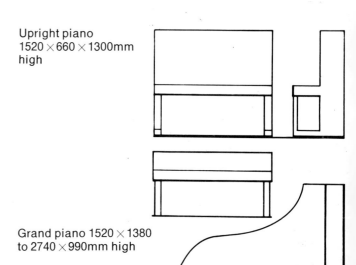

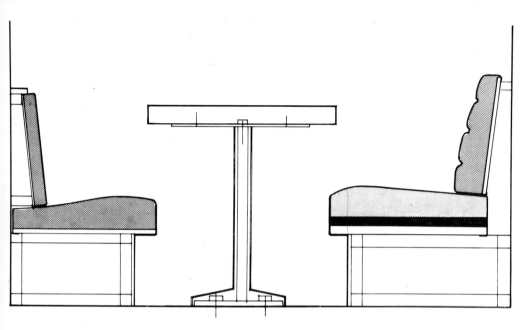

BANQUETTE SEATING

Standard banquette seating (left) with 100mm single grade foam, width 450mm

Luxury bench seating (right) with 100mm soft foam on 25mm hard foam, width 500mm and contoured back

Fixed banquette table for four 1200 × 600 × 760mm high with rounded corners for ease of access
Mild steel support bolted to floor with chromed cover

In a high-priced restaurant comfort will be of vital importance and soft upholstery materials should be considered. Buttoning and fluting give added luxury and deep seats help to give support. Springing is of great importance and a sprung seat will give greater comfort than a foam one. If foam is used then 100mm of soft foam with a 25 mm layer of medium foam over it is best. The normal height is 460 to 480mm but when a soft seat is used this should be increased to about 500mm.

In lounges, bars and reception areas similar criteria apply, with the exception that seating can be about 400mm high and, where people are expected to stay for long periods, it is essential to consider the shape of the back to give proper lumbar, and possibly head, support. These considerations apply to loose furniture as well as fixed seating.

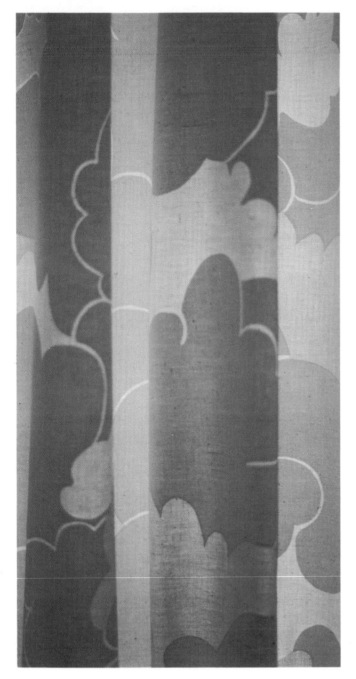

An enormous range of fabrics exists from which to choose a design that complements the facilities. Texture is an important quality in fabrics

Ceramic tiles are a relatively expensive and permanent covering for floors and walls, but they can be very striking if used imaginatively

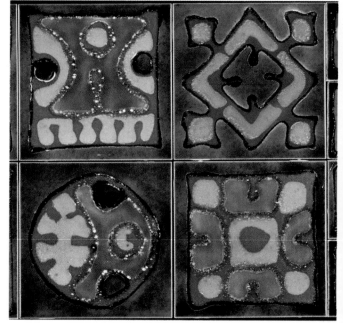

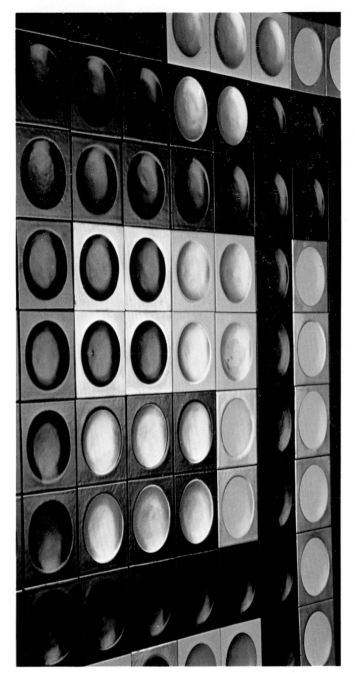

Plain or patterned rugs and carpets can be used in areas with moderate traffic

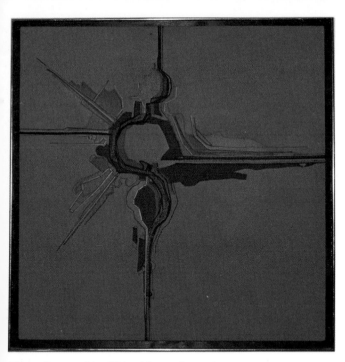

Works of art provide additional interest for guests

89

Tableware

The very strong impression given by table settings means that great care should be taken over the choice of cutlery, china, glassware, mats, linen and other accoutrements for dining rooms and restaurants. The small things in an interior play a vital part, particularly when they are under close scrutiny by the customer, and can raise the status of an establishment above mediocrity, and even become a talking point at the table or the bar.

Each item should be chosen for its fitness for purpose, both in shape and material; its compatibility with the rest of the interior; its cost; its expected life; its maintenance costs; the ease with which it can be stored or stacked; its ease of replacement; and its hygiene in use.

The type of usage must be defined from the outset as being the most severe treatment by unskilled or semi-skilled labour working under extreme pressure, no matter how efficient supervision and management are likely to be.

Tableware is used not only in restaurants and hotel dining rooms but also for banquets. Banquet requirements are different from many restaurant requirements in that the whole of the banquet is served in a very short space of time and soiled dishes are removed after each course at great speed. In this case a reduction in noise is an advantage but directional patterns on crockery (coats of arms, for instance) can be a disadvantage as alignment is impossible in a hurry.

Tableware used in hotels should be able to be washed both mechanically and by hand. Bases of cups, plates and so on should therefore not have a recess that will collect water and drip over other items that have already been dried. It is also important to avoid designs with sharp edges and corners, complicated mouldings, protruding feet, dirt traps of all sorts, and unnecessary moving parts if denting, bending, scratching, chipping, breaking, crazing and staining are to be avoided. All materials should be impervious to water, in spite of some traditions to the contrary, like wooden salad bowls. Ease of cleaning or polishing should be noted in particular and all unavoidable protrusions such as handles, spouts, lids and so on should be easily cleaned and strongly attached to avoid damage. Stability and

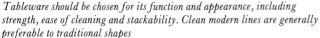
Tableware should be chosen for its function and appearance, including strength, ease of cleaning and stackability. Clean modern lines are generally preferable to traditional shapes

stackability are also important, as is lightness. Rationalise where possible and ensure that lids, for example, can be interchanged for different sizes of teapot.

The hotelier is constantly searching for materials that will reduce breakage rates and it is to be hoped that manufacturers will continue to experiment with new materials to overcome their disadvantages – plastics, for example, tend to scratch and discolour more quickly than traditional ceramics. In general terms, the materials used should not taint food or drink; should be highly resistant to chipping, cracking, crazing, pitting, blotching and breakage; should have a smooth surface which will not scratch or corrode; should be capable of passing repeatedly through washing machines at temperatures of up to 85°C without being affected by strong detergents; should be capable of maintaining its colour and any decorations on it; should not absorb moisture; should be able to have handles, knobs, etc, firmly attached to it; should be a poor conductor of heat (depending on the article concerned); should be light in weight; should require a minimum of replating or polishing; should retain an edge without sharpening

(if used for cutting purposes); and should be pleasing to look at and, if used for drinking vessels or eating, feel pleasant to the touch.

The shapes of pots and jugs used for tea, hot water, coffee and hot milk should be easily recognised by guests and staff so that they know what it is they should contain. Tea must infuse at a temperature as near boiling point as possible, and as rapidly as possible, which is why broad, shallow teapots are to be preferred to narrow ones, such as those used for coffee. Teapots are often heated on hotplates and so an insulated base is a disadvantage. A fixed, efficient strainer should be incorporated into the design of the teapot and be easily cleaned. For coffee pots, milk jugs, water and cream jugs the shape is less important but most of the other requirements apply. The lids should remain in place when the liquid is being poured; hinged lids should be strongly fixed and they have the advantage of not being possible to lose. On the other hand, pots with lids attached may be impossible to stack and harder to clean. Detachable lids are easily cleaned and can be replaced separately if damaged.

The table on page 111 shows preferred sizes for some items of tableware, including carafes and wine jugs. The hotel trade prefers carafes to decanters because decanters are expensive and very difficult to clean.

Beer or lager jugs should not have a pinched lip like water jugs because they will not need to retain ice cubes. The eventual requirement here may be for a government-certified jug of a certain capacity.

Cups should ideally be manufactured in exact sizes of four, six, seven and eight ounces when filled to within 5mm of the rim. Handles should be designed with a good bearing on the body as this is the weakest point for breakage. A loop handle allows space for the index finger up to the first joint. Cups should be designed so that they can be stacked without chipping. Rims should be as thin as possible in accordance with strength. Heat retention depends on the diameter and height of cups and preference should be given to tall cups, which hold heat well. Tea and coffee cups should be six, seven or eight ounce, and the coffee cup a demi-tasse size of about four ounces.

Wine and spirit glasses should be perfectly transparent and colourless so that the colour and clarity of their contents are not impaired. So far the only satisfactory material is glass.

For wine, the diameter of the rim should not exceed any other part of the bowl and many wine connoisseurs insist that it should be smaller to retain the bouquet of the wine. Champagne should also be served in a tulip or flute shaped glass and not the shallow saucer type. It should be possible to hold the glass for red wines so that the hand can warm the contents, but the opposite is true for white wines. The drawings on page 111 show the appropriate shapes and sizes.

For plates, saucers and bowls, the hotel trade generally prefers a rolled edge to resist chipping, in spite of the fact that this looks less elegant. The same is true to some extent for glasses as well. It is best to avoid very flat plates where small quantities of food look lost and liquids are easily spilt. Overall diameter should be between 150–200mm and not larger, otherwise they will not fit into many dishwashers. Sideplates should be large enough to hold a roll and butter and should also be suitable for use as a base plate for a demi-tasse and saucer. Plates should be able to be stacked in piles of 30.

Sizes marked on the base of plates might be an advantage and soup plates, bowls, etc, should be similarly marked with their capacities. Sizes currently used in hotels are 6, $6\frac{1}{2}$, 7, $7\frac{1}{2}$, 8, $8\frac{1}{2}$, 9, $9\frac{1}{2}$ and 10 ounces, but rationalisation is recommended for each establishment.

The shape and size of saucers is very much determined by the type of cup used. It is important, however, that the cup should be held so that it does not slip around on the saucer, and that spoons lie on it without slipping off. Saucers should be able to be stacked in 30s, like plates.

Salad bowls should be round, with a diameter between 200–300mm. They should be sufficiently deep and wide to allow salad to be tossed without danger of spilling and they should also be stackable and impervious to dressings.

A bowl is needed for fruit with sauces or ice cream, and this is usually stood on a 175mm plate. Stemmed bowls have the disadvantage of being more easily broken, unstable, hard to clean and unstackable. A good design can be used for fruit, ices, cereals, etc.

The sugar basins and slop bowls can be identical, between 65–100mm diameter.

There is an occasional need for a double-skinned bowl that can be filled with either hot water or crushed ice for use with souffles, fruit compotes, fish cocktails, fruit salads, peach melbas and so forth. It should be about 250mm diameter and have a flat base to the lining to facilitate the preparation of the food.

Flat covered dishes should be rectangular, with roll radius corners, which are best for ease of service and hygiene. A rectangular shape stacks and stands more easily than oval and it is also easier to arrange a number of equal portions on a rectangular dish. However, gateaux call for smaller, round dishes. Dishes of this type should be about 35mm deep and their length should vary from 150 to 600mm in 50mm intervals. Width should generally be about three fifths of length throughout.

Dishes divided into two compartments are also useful and should be 150, 200 and 250mm long.

Flat covers should be designed so that they can also be used as serving dishes. They should stack and should also be able to be stacked when they are in position on top of dishes.

Special tableware may be more appropriate in expensive restaurants

Raised covers should be deep enough to accommodate joints of meat and poultry. The depth should be in proportion to size up to about 150mm. They must stack and be easily lifted in one hand.

Sauce boats should be designed both for pouring and for use with a ladle or spoon. When in use they should stand, either one or two at a time, on plates of appropriate size. The sauce boats themselves should be of three, six and twelve fluid ounces capacity. Stability is an important consideration and handles must be strong.

Bread and fruit dishes serve a dual purpose. They should be easy to clean and not have legs.

Toast racks should be stackable and simple in design. They should hold various thicknesses of toast, four or six pieces each, and be easily cleaned. Solid partitions are to be avoided. Air must be able to get to both sides of the toast

White wine is kept ready for serving at the temperature at which it is drunk, 10°C. An insulated container will prevent the wine getting warm and there should be two sizes, one for half bottles and the other large enough to take a tall hock bottle or a magnum of champagne.

Trays should be light, strong, silent in use, hygienic, stackable and with a non-slip surface. A number of shapes and sizes will be needed and they should have raised edges to contain spills. For early morning tea a size between 350 by 250 and 400 by 250mm will be needed. For breakfast in bedrooms the tray should be larger – between 500 by 375 and 610 by 400mm – depending on the capacity of washing-up machines and service lifts. A round tray of about 300mm diameter is useful for serving drinks. Some hotels need trays with 200mm foldable legs for bedroom use, but with well designed spaces for trays at the bedside this is not really necessary.

Salt and pepper containers should be of good appearance, be easy to fill and clean, and resist corrosion and damage. Mustard pots should also be easily cleaned and have a minimum number of parts. A lid will be needed to keep the contents moist. The normal size is between two and three fluid ounces. Mustard made with vinegar can be served in larger pots.

Individual butter dishes will be needed and they should be about one half ounce capacity. A larger, shallow dish will also be needed, about 120mm diameter.

Egg cups with integral saucer-like bases present washing-up difficulties, particularly in machines. Egg cups without feet are to be preferred and must be stable in use.

The appearance of ash trays is important, but their function is even more so. A cigarette resting on an ash tray must not fall on its end and extinguish itself with an unpleasant smell, nor fall outwards where it may burn a tablecloth or table top. Ash trays should also be easy to clean. Several different sizes will be needed.

Cutlery in hotels and restaurants is subject to heavy wear and must stand up to mechanical washing. Difficulties arise if handles are hollow and can be punctured so that water drips over the user. Bone, plastics or nylon handles can discolour and become loose. The shape of cutlery should be comfortable, well balanced, well angled and pleasant to look at. Knives for table use, for fish, for cheese, for cheese serving, for butter and for counter use will be needed. Fish knives are traditionally made of silver or plate, but stainless steel is equally satisfactory. The only distinction is that the fish knife should not be as sharp as other knives and that it should have a broad blade.

Four-pronged forks are easier to use than three-pronged ones, but they are more difficult to clean. Strength is important. Different types are required for desserts, fish, fruit, pastries (or tea) and table use. It is a hotel requirement that up to ten pairs of knives and forks can be laid on a plate in such a way that they are not likely to fall off.

There should be different types of spoon for coffee, desserts, mustard, soup, tea, and table use, as well as ladles for sauces and soup. Spoons with a shallow bowl can give rise to drips if they are over-filled. Coffee spoons must not be so long that they will not balance on the saucer.

In all tableware, the hotelier must assess the need for different sizes of utensil. It may be possible (and cheaper) to have one medium-sized type of knife to combine the functions of a table knife and cheese knife, for example. The same is true for forks, and a combined tea and coffee spoon is almost always preferred by staff as there is no chance of picking the wrong size by mistake. Table spoons used for serving food must be bigger than dessert spoons and a round-shaped soup spoon is also preferred, rather than doubling up with the serving spoon.

A decision must be made on whether to use tablecloths or just bare tops to the tables, perhaps in plastics laminate. If cloths are chosen the design must be selected carefully, bearing in mind colour, wear resistance, ease of cleaning, fabric quality and treatment of the edging. Their appearance should be linked to the restaurant's theme where appropriate. Napkins should, if possible, always be cloth: paper reduces the quality of the establishment dramatically.

Tablecloths are traditionally made from linen, but there is now a wide range of materials, including man-made fabrics. Their relative characteristics are that linen is good to look at, resistant to wear, but expensive; cotton is cheaper but is less wear-resistant, although it can be blended with linen or man-made fibres; nylon and terylene look rather different but can be blended with cotton and are resistant to creasing.

In terms of colour and pattern, coloured fabrics are more likely to fade, will be more difficult to clean and can fade by different amount, so that tablecloths and napkins fail to match. Plain or decorative weaves can be used, including damasks and other designs.

Linen can be purchased or hired. The stock requirement should not be underestimated: about six times the number of tables and place settings with a five year replacement cycle or 20 per cent replacement per year is about right.

The design of table mats is important and can be used to extend the graphic design of the establishment through pictures or lettering. Individually designed table mats are quite cheap. Plastics laminate is more durable, but also more expensive.

Works of art

Hotels and restaurants can provide extra items of interest to guests by showing selected works of art. These can provide focal points within the establishment and need not be an expensive capital investment. The hotel or restaurant can be a facility for local artists to show paintings for sale and this can be a small source of revenue. However, the owner must be selective and invite only those whose paintings are of good quality and contribute to the interior as a whole.

Never before has the human eye been subjected to so many images, not only from paintings, graphics, photographs and sculpture, but also from the bombardment of television. Any visual material must therefore be carefully considered.

As far as pictures are concerned the range is vast, from lesser historical works to modern paintings and pop art. They may be miniatures or cover whole walls, in subtle colours or in vibrant patterns. Security will be a problem if valuable works of art are used but this is usually not necessary and would be hard to justify. Local artists, whether contemporary or from the past, provide a good link between the building and its neighbourhood. Framing is very important and can make even quite insignificant works of art contribute a great deal to an interior. Many lithographs and screen prints by well-known artists can be bought and these, since they are usually produced in a limited run, are much better quality than ordinary reproductions. With the opportunity to buy good prints of this kind and relatively cheap originals, it should not be necessary to resort to reproductions. If they are required, however, avoid expensive prints signed on the stone as these are no more valuable than good reproductions sold by fine art dealers.

Sculpture and three-dimensional works of art can be used in key positions and, as with pictures, can be either traditional or modern. They can be made of stone, bronze, glass fibre, steel, glass, timber or other materials. Sculpture is often expensive because of the high cost of the materials used.

Embroidery, collage and sculptural weaving can also be used as important elements in an interior. Works of this kind, which fall between craft and art, can be extremely interesting compositions in two or three

dimensions which produce a variety of wonderful and unusual effects.

Obviously, this choice is not intended to be comprehensive; the possible range is infinite and the manager or owner has immense scope in choosing items that help to produce a personality for the building. Modern materials provide a continual challenge to the art world and this lends a further dimension to the interest of interiors. If movement is required, for example, there are paintings and sculptures that move, such as mobiles and kinetic sculptures.

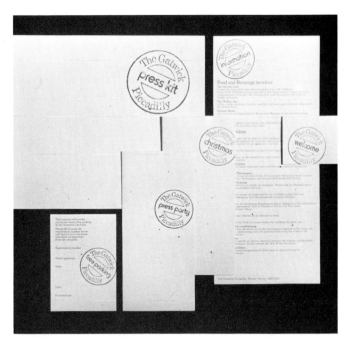

Direction signs and notices form a very important element of the building and must be clear and well designed. Properly chosen and laid out lettering in appropriate colours and in suitable positions will add to the quality of the interior as much as bad signing will detract from it. For emergency signs it will be necessary to consult the fire officer, but slight re-positioning of signs (with his approval) will often improve appearance without detracting from their functional purpose. Consider also their impact when illuminated at night.

There are also many other printed documents to be considered. Large hotels may find it helpful to produce a staff manual setting down the aims of the management, the statement of policy required under the Health and Safety at Work Act covering fire escapes, fire extinguishers and other hazards. This manual can be extended to talk about working conditions, to explain facilities available to the staff, their approach to customers, and information on the neighbourhood, including useful addresses, transport and places of entertainment. A similar list will be of use to guests.

Graphic design

The first communication between the client and an establishment is likely to be through the printed word in the form of a brochure or on arrival at the information desk. A hotel must therefore decide on what impression is to be given in terms of its house style and impact, so visual appearance is most important. Guests will react to this initial contact and will be to some extent conditioned by it. This will affect their response to the service, the accommodation and the price.

Care should be taken to design the whole range of graphics in the hotel to give continuity in typeface, size and general appearance of printed material and signs. This will give an impression of care and attention to detail which will be appreciated.

Brochures should give an indication of the type of building and the facilities provided, presenting this information in a decorative and imaginative way. The brochure can include local attractions where appropriate. With rising postal costs and the need to send brochures abroad it may be necessary to consider a small brochure of a single folded page of similar quality to the main brochure, for air mail use. Specialised brochures may be needed if specific facilities are offered, such as conference centres or catering for parties. Prices should be avoided in brochures of this type, which may have to last for some time before reprinting; a separate price list will be cheaper in the long run.

Menus and wine lists should be attractively laid out and both these items can give an individual personality to a restaurant or dining room, including perhaps a few lines on the historical connections of the building or nearby features. The menu design must be easy to read. Guests may like to be allowed to take an attractive menu away with them.

Letter paper, envelopes and postcards need similar care over their design. Lightweight versions should be available for airmail use. Colour and design are of great importance and the whole image of the hotel will be enhanced by a consistent design linking these items and the brochure. If elaborate coloured designs are used this will involve expensive printing. This could be reserved for special occasions and a simplified form used for normal correspondence and for use by guests.

A selection of co-ordinated graphic material for use in one hotel group

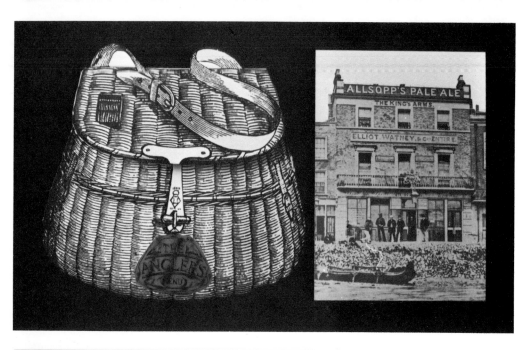

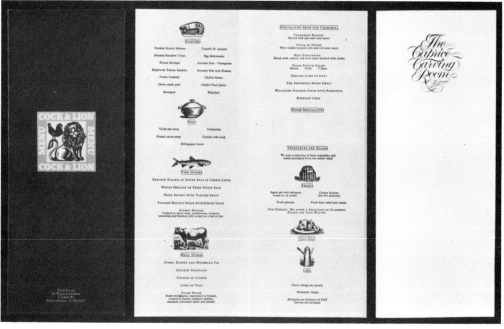

THE
White Horse
BILL of FARE

To start

Prawns
blended with tarragon
flavoured mayonnaise

Fried Whitebait

Melon
with Port wine

Smoked Scotch Salmon

Cheddar, Anchovy & Bacon Tart

Surrey Chicken Broth

Game Soup

Our Selection of potted meats
game, poultry and smoked fish

Savoury Omelette
chopped ham, shallots
and fresh herbs

Fish

Trout
cooked in leek leaves
with dill butter

Whole Dover Sole
fried or grilled with
Parsley butter

Herrings
pan fried in butter
with oatmeal, served
with Gooseberry sauce

Meat & poultry

Dorking Hot-Pot
made with chicken, ham,
pork sausage, fresh vegetables
and herbs

Pot Roasted Half Chicken
with lemon and tarragon stuffing

Roast Quail
stuffed with mushrooms and
a sauce of grapes and
Port wine

Prime Sirloin Steak
grilled in butter and
served with a spiced sauce

Jugged Hare
with Redcurrant jelly

Kidneys
grilled and flamed in
Brandy, served with
Rosemary butter sauce

Ham
sliced and fried with
eggs and mushrooms

Vegetables

A selection of freshly cooked
vegetables and potatoes is
included with the main course

Cold table

Boiled Ham

Spiced Beef

Our own Chicken Pie

Sweets & Puddings

Syllabub
a blend of lemons, sherry,
Brandy and cream

Banana Fritters
with Apricot sauce

Waffles

Apple Pie
with cream

The Sweet Trolley

A selection of Dairy Ice Creams
served with hot
Butterscotch or Rum
and Raisin sauce

English cheeses

Stilton

Cheddar

Double Gloucester

With fresh fruit

May we suggest
some Vintage Port
with bowl of nuts

......Glass

Coffee

TIPPING: For the convenience of our guests
10% is added to all accounts to cover service and
all gratuities. Further tipping, therefore, is unnecessary

*Menus, wine lists and uniforms are all important points of contact with guests
and can give individuality to a restaurant or dining room*

This folding menu carries through the design theme of the restaurant

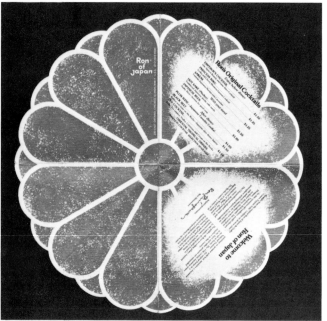

Screens and partitions

Screens and partitions are important items these days as plans become more open and spaces need to be divided. Considerable emphasis has been placed on demountable partitions; the illustrations show some types of partition that are very flexible in use. Tall movable screens, usually zig-zag in plan form to give stability and in fairly small sections so that they can be lifted and stored easily, are only moderately good acoustically. Low solid screens can be used to give privacy when sitting down without obstructing the view when standing or moving about. They are a development of the type of screen used in open-plan offices and their acoustic properties are generally poor. Decorative screens can be straight, curved, or shaped to give a sense of division but are also poor acoustically. Sliding and folding partitions can be solid or movable in limited directions depending on materials and tracks used. They can be covered in soft materials like hessian, wallpaper, leathercloth and so on. They can be made reasonably soundproof, depending on their weight and the treatment at floor and ceiling. Concertina walls can be single or double shell, sliding or folding, and may be covered in a wide range of materials although most are produced in vinyl.

Panel walls and movable walls consisting of individual panels operated independently and fixed in a ceiling track can have pneumatic devices for soundproofing and can be very flexible in use if the track is carefully designed and fitted.

Security is often a problem in hotels and restaurants and to comply with licensing requirements consideration must be given to screening off bars. Decorative grilles and screens need to be carefully designed to fit into bars and canopies so that they do not disrupt the quality of the space when the bar is open. Similar grilles can be used for bank facilities, shops and reception areas in large hotels where security is necessary.

SCREENS AND PARTITIONS

Independent moveable screens are often not more than 2000mm high and are stable if curved or folded. Flat panels need feet. Screens can be covered in most materials

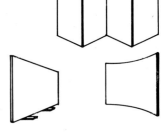

Sliding or folding screens can be made of timber and either painted or covered in a variety of materials

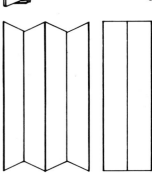

Collapsible vinyl-covered screens will require soundproofing if they are used to divided two occupied areas

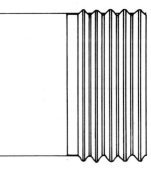

A number of different track arrangements can be made for folding back, sliding or stacking timber screens to divide large spaces

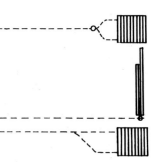

Maintenance

A modern building is a complex assembly of a great variety of components, materials and services. This section is intended to help with the care and maintenance of buildings, fittings and interiors.

The initial design of the building can help considerably in reducing the maintenance problem, and function has been stressed throughout this book. A considerable amount can be done just by common sense and there is an ongoing need for regular inspection and appraisal of the interior and exterior of the building. A well cared-for building produces a good reaction from clients and it is possible to absorb experiments in decoration that have failed and avoid them in future when renewing surfaces or replacing fittings.

Good design pays and it will be worth spending a little extra from time to time in certain areas to achieve the right effect. Maintenance for its own sake cannot be used as an excuse for a dull building.

New buildings or additions need to dry out and ventilation is also important in old buildings. A good circulation of air is essential and this is particularly true for cupboards and small rooms without a lot of natural air movement in order to prevent mildew growth. Shrinkage cracks will appear if excessive heat and low humidity are maintained.

Condensation occurs when warm, moist air comes into contact with cold surfaces. During the initial drying-out process it is likely that the air in a building will be more moist than usual, so it is essential that good ventilation is maintained. Even if a building is insulated to modern standards, condensation is likely to occur on windows, on walls of unheated rooms, and occasionally on exposed external walls under severe weather conditions. To reduce condensation to a minimum it is important to maintain a warm, but not too hot, temperature and to keep all rooms ventilated.

When brickwork dries out it sometimes produces on its surface a deposit of white salts left by the evaporating water. On outside walls these show initially as patchy white marks which are soon dissolved away by rain. The same thing can occur in old buildings that have an inadequate damp-proof course, flashings, or roof drainage so that walls become wet and attract a deposit of salt. On the inside of the building the salts will show on the surface of fair-faced brickwork and even through plaster. This does little harm, although it looks unsightly and frequently makes paintwork blister or peel. The salts can be removed simply by washing with a warm, damp cloth, but they will continue to appear until the brickwork is entirely dry. At this point redecoration can be carried out without fear of further damage.

In recent years mildew has become a problem. It will occur under suitable conditions on timber, plaster and in particular emulsion painted surfaces where there is some dampness. It is particularly likely in small closed rooms, cupboards and in corners where air movement is poor. In most cases it can quite simply be wiped off the surface of the paintwork using a solution of domestic bleach in warm water. In the case of new buildings, pictures and mirrors should be fixed clear of the walls to allow air to circulate behind them. All mirrors should be of steamproof quality.

Failure to provide regular care and maintenance can, in the long run, prove expensive when major breakdowns result in both inconvenience and capital cost. It is generally accepted that all paintwork should be redecorated externally every three years and internally every five. These are maximum figures and frequently in hotels and restaurants where wear is heavy the period should be shorter. Service equipment is often complex and will require regular maintenance. Contracts for servicing can generally be arranged.

Light fittings are designed to take lamps of a given power and great care should be taken that the correct lamps are used and that this figure is never exceeded. The danger of fire and electrical failure if high-powered lamps are used in fittings not designed for them is considerable. In general electrical appliances should be connected in accordance with electricity board recommendations. Oversize fuses should not be used as this can be dangerous.

Many doors in the building will be designed as fire doors for safety reasons. These must be kept closed if they are to be of any use and fittings to close them must therefore be kept effective. Doors of this kind must not be wedged or fixed open unless they are controlled by a fire detector and an automatic closing device.

Coverings and nosings to staircases must be kept in good repair and well fixed to prevent tripping.

The following summary gives details of how to maintain most of the materials and finishes commonly met with in building of this type:

WINDOW CLEANING

Glass	Wash down with clean water and leather with damp chamois leather.	Weekly

WINDOW FRAMES

Aluminium, anodised aluminium, stainless steel, lacquered metal	Clean with warm soapy water, applied with a cloth or leather. Dry and polish with a soft dry cloth.	Quarterly
Bronze	Apply thin coating of paraffin oil, allow to dry thoroughly and polish with a soft cloth.	Quarterly

IRONMONGERY

Anodised aluminium, chromium plate, lacquered metal	Clean with warm soapy water applied with a cloth or leather. Dry and polish with soft dry cloth	Weekly
Bronze	Apply thin coating of paraffin oil, allow to dry thoroughly and polish with a soft cloth.	Weekly
Brass	Apply thin coating of metal polish. Allow to dry and polish with a soft cloth.	Weekly
Stainless steel	Clean with warm soapy water and dry off with a leather and polish with a soft cloth	Weekly

WALLS

Fairface brickwork	Brush down with a stiff dry brush.	Annually
Cement glaze	Wash down with warm water and weak detergent. Rinse with clean water and leather down with chamois leather.	Annually
Glazed wall tiles, glazed brickwork, granite, vitreous enamelled panels	Wash down with warm water and weak detergent. Rinse with clean water and polish with a soft cloth.	
Plastics (Formica, Wareite)	Remove dirty marks with cellulose polish (Karpol). Wipe over with a damp cloth and dry with a soft cloth.	Annually
Polished hardwood	Apply reviving polish with a damp leather, rub well in and leave no surplus	Annually
Marble	Wash down with warm soapy water. Rinse with clean water and dry with a soft cloth. Apply a thin coating of wax furniture cream and polish with a soft cloth.	Annually
PVC coated fabric	Wash down with warm water and weak detergent. Remove dirty marks by brushing with a soft brush and rinse with clean water.	Annually

FLOORS

Coloured asphalt	Apply water/wax emulsion polish with a damp cloth or mop and when dry, lightly buff with a polishing machine. Remove accumulations of polish with detergent in hot water, rinse with clean water and dry, reapply polish. Remove dirty marks with a damp cloth or mop.	Fortnightly
Linoleum	Scuff marks which cannot be removed by this method may be removed by light rubbing with a fine steel wool pad dipped in liquid polish. Apply paste or liquid wax polish, rub into surface with a dry cloth and, when dry, buff with a polishing machine. A water/wax emulsion polish gives greater non-slip properties. Apply with a damp cloth or mop and, when dry, buff with a polishing machine. Remove accumulations of polish with detergent in hot water, rinse with clean water and, when dry, re-apply polish or dry rub with a fine steel wool pad and re-apply polish.	Fortnightly
Rubber	Apply water/wax emulsion polish with a damp cloth or mop and, when dry, lightly buff with a polishing machine. Remove accumulations of polish with paste cleaner using warm water, rinse with clean water and, when dry, re-apply polish.	Fortnightly
Terrazzo	Lightly scrub with warm water using a gritty cleansing powder, rinse with clean water and squeegee to remove surplus water.	Weekly
Thermoplastic tiles and PVC tiles	Remove dirty marks with a damp cloth or mop. Scuff marks which cannot be removed by this method may be removed by light rubbing with a fine steel wool pad dipped in liquid polish. Apply water/wax emulsion polish with a damp cloth or mop and, when dry, lightly buff with a polishing machine. Remove accumulations of polish with detergent in hot water, rinse with clean water and, when dry, re-apply polish.	Fortnightly

Note: Polishes containing turpentine, white spirit or similar solvents must not be used.

106

Hardwood block or strip	Apply paste or liquid wax polish, rub into surface with a dry cloth and, when dry buff with a polishing machine. Remove accumulations of polish by dry rubbing with a medium steel wool pad or wet rub with a medium steel wool pad, dipped in liquid polish and, when dry, buff with a polishing machine.	Fortnightly
Quarry tiles, concrete tiles	Wash with warm water and detergent and rinse with clean water. Squeegee to remove surplus water.	Weekly
Concrete granolithic	Scrub with warm water and detergent. Rinse with clean water. Squeegee to remove surplus water.	Weekly
Carpets	Vacuum clean regularly in the direction of the pile. Dry clean carpets using only shampoos marked as complying with British Standard 4088. Note: under no circumstances should carpets be saturated during dry cleaning.	Daily
Stain removal	Prompt and correct treatment removes many stains but wrong treatment may only serve to increase the	

damage. In cases where there is doubt or severe damage, it is advisable to seek skilled assistance. Remove substances spilt quickly before it penetrates the carpet pile.

INTERIOR PAINTWORK

Washable distemper	Brush lightly with a dry fine hair broom.	Weekly
Gloss paint, semi-gloss paint, flat oil paint, emulsion paint	Wash down with warm water and weak detergent. Rinse with clean water and leather down with chamois leather.	Annually

FURNISHINGS

PVC upholstery	Clean with warm soapy water, applied with a soft brush. Rinse with clean water and dry with a soft cloth.	Monthly
Fabric upholstery	Vacuum clean and brush with a stiff upholstery brush.	Monthly
Polished wood	Apply wax furniture cream and polish with a soft dry cloth.	Fortnightly
Painted wood, painted metal	Wash down with warm water and weak detergent. Rinse with clean water and polish with a soft cloth.	Annually

TOILETS

Sanitary fittings	Clean with porcelain cleaning powder and

	warm water. Rinse with clean water and polish with a soft cloth.	Daily
Copper	Apply thin coating of metal polish. Allow to dry and polish with a soft cloth.	Weekly
Stainless steel	Clean with warm soapy water and dry off with a leather and polish with a soft cloth.	Weekly
Mirrors	Wash down with clean water and leather with damp chamois leather.	Monthly
Chromium plate	Clean with warm soapy water applied with a cloth or leather. Dry and polish with a soft dry cloth.	Weekly

Carpets should be treated gently for the first month or so, avoiding excessive vacuum cleaning or shampooing. Wear can be made more even by rearranging furniture and, in the case of carpet squares and stair carpets, moving them twice a year. Stair carpets are laid with the pile facing down the flight of stairs and should never be turned round. If carpets are cleaned it is often better to do this while they are in place to avoid shrinkage and distortion.

In the case of alcohol, fruit stains, grass stains, ink (except ball point pens, which need methylated spirits with a little white vinegar added to prevent spreading) and food stains, remove as much of the stain as possible with a knife. For wine, remove the surplus first. Then prepare one teaspoonful of white vinegar to a pint of diluted carpet shampoo and apply with a sponge or absorbent cloth, rubbing gently and repeating until the stain is removed. Finish with clean water, leaving the pile in the correct direction. For coffee, tea, milk, grease, paint, shoe polish and soot, after removing as much as possible with a vacuum cleaner, proceed with the treatment as above and follow this, if the stain has not been removed, with a dry cleaning solvent on an absorbent cloth in accordance with the manufacturer's instructions with good ventilation.

Salt should be removed with a vacuum cleaner or brush as it can affect the colour of the carpet. Mop up small amounts of spilt water but for large-scale flooding call in professional cleaners immediately and do not allow the carpet to dry as distortion will take place and the discolouration will be difficult to remove.

High standards of maintenance and cleanliness rapidly communicate themselves to guests

7 SERVICES AND EQUIPMENT

Staff and service areas are vital parts of the building. Time and effort spent on improving working conditions will reduce strain on staff and therefore help to improve the relationships between them and the guests.

Starting with the reception desk, a careful appraisal of what is required here will help the designer to produce a satisfactory solution. Ergonomics are a critical factor in its design, particularly if small numbers of staff are available and the work load fluctuates. The design must cope with the peak busy periods. Points to be considered include:

1 Number of staff available
2 Appearance and style required
3 Possibility of one person operation in which the receptionist can operate telephones, receive guests, issue keys, issue bills and accounts, and answer guests' queries
4 If in a large or medium-sized establishment, the size of counter needed for the numbers of staff and guests envisaged, and its relationship to them
5 Desk height, either for standing or sitting. If large numbers of guests use the desk at peak periods it will be easier and more comfortable for the receptionist to work in a standing position or on a tall stool
6 Keys, which are best kept linked to pigeon holes for messages, passports etc. This system can be extended to include accounts if required
7 Billing can be either manual or electric. Space should be provided for the necessary equipment
8 Storage will be needed for literature, postcards, guests' valuables etc, and should therefore include a safe
9 Paging and call system, if required
10 Telephone system

The reception desk is the nerve centre of the establishment and does a lot to set the tone of the whole building.

RECEPTION DESKS

Desk for standing guest and staff
Work surface height for guest 1050mm
Work surface height for staff 850mm with space under top shelf for privacy and storage of small items

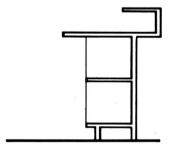

Desk for seated guest and staff 720mm high with adequate width and knee space

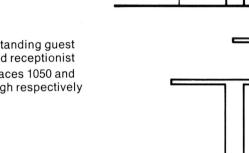

Desk for standing guest and seated receptionist
Work surfaces 1050 and 720mm high respectively

Storage

Too little consideration is generally given to storage of all sorts when planning and a careful study of future needs could avoid many problems. Correctly positioned stores of the right size will save time and improve control of goods and materials. Points to be considered include:

1 Type of storage needed
2 Provision of central, security storage
3 Provision of peripheral storage
4 Need for walk-in storage with shelves or cupboards
5 Structural provisions for major storage weights
6 Provision of flexible storage, with fixed or adjustable shelving
7 Type of shelving material
8 Dimensions. The following sizes are intended as a guide only

STORAGE

Folded linen

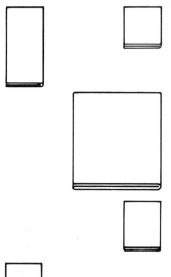

Pillow-cases	255 × 255mm
Blankets	610 × 610mm
Bath towels	305 × 255mm
Face towels	205 × 205mm
Tablecloths	405 × 255mm

Clothing

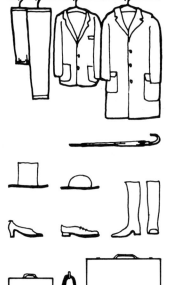

Coats	600 × 1360mm
Suits	600 × 1000mm
Skirts and dresses	600 × 800 to 1360mm
Boots	400 × 450mm high
Shoes	400 × 150mm high
Briefcases	450 × 200mm
Cases	430 × 760 × 260mm
Small trunks	1020 × 540 × 300mm

Linen store

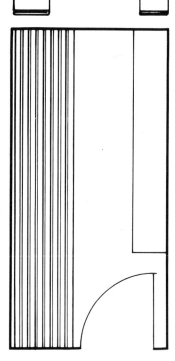

Shelves for blankets and sheets 610mm wide

Shelves for pillow-cases and towels 305mm wide

Bottom shelf should be 75mm from floor

Next shelf 610mm above

Other shelves spaced at 350mm

TABLEWARE

Wine and spirit glasses
Height 70 to 140mm
Diameter 35 to 90mm

Plates
Circular 175, 230, 255mm
Oval dishes 355 × 255mm
and 405 × 305mm

Long drink glasses
Height 115 to 165mm
Diameter (with handles)
70 to 140mm

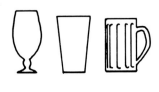

Beer bottles and cans
Height 205 to 280mm
Diameter 65 to 75mm

Wine bottles
Height 355mm
Diameter 90mm

**Cider flagons,
magnum bottles
and ice buckets**
Height 320mm
Diameter 185mm

Spirit bottles and soda
Height 330mm
Diameter up to 110mm

Barrels
Height 450 to 1050mm
Diameter 300 to 750mm

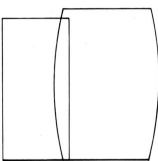

111

Wines, beers and spirits

The storage of wine needs to be considered carefully. Wines take between three and twenty years to develop in storage and some, including vintage ports, take considerably longer. There are five main points that should be considered:

1 Temperature. Violent changes of temperature must be avoided. A room with a constant temperature between 10 to 13°C is ideal, but if the temperature rises slowly above this to moderate levels very little harm will be done
2 Darkness. Wine should be stored away from direct daylight and certainly away from sunlight, which will upset the natural development of the wine
3 Cleanliness. A good, ventilated space is to be preferred as it avoids smells, which can contaminate the wine, and the growth of harmful bacteria
4 Freedom from vibration
5 Capital cost. The quality of the storage will determine how long the wine can be kept and, therefore, the type and price of wine served

Further problems exist in connection with serving wine. It is important that red wines are served at room temperature, but they must not be warmed violently or rapidly. Dipping bottles in water must be avoided and, if possible, the wine should be allowed to breathe, uncorked, before serving. White wine should be served slightly chilled, again avoiding rapidly changing its temperature. It will therefore be helpful to have a selection of wines available at the correct temperature for choice by the clientele. The choice is really between having a very big wine list and a more moderate one of good quality. Bin storage for wine will have to be arranged according to the quantities of each wine needed, as shown in the diagram. It is not necessary to have individual storage for each bottle unless there is a wide range of wines with only a few bottles of each.

Many of the conditions applying to wines are equally important for the storage of beers and spirits. There should be adequate thermal insulation, even temperature control at about 12°C, clean and hygienic conditions, and a strategic position for ease of delivery, return of empties and bar service.

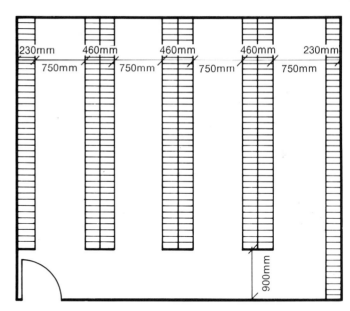

WINE STORAGE **Large wine store with metal racks**

Small wine store with bins gives maximum capacity in small space. Each bin contains one wine
With 600mm depth double rows of bottles can be accomodated

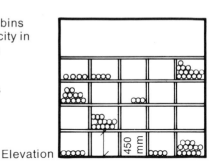

Elevation

Plan

Small wine store with stone, slate or concrete bins

Cleaning equipment

Storage of equipment for cleaning and other purposes will depend on the capital available, the size of the establishment, and the number of staff who use it. Consider whether it will be better to have a central store for vacuum cleaners, polishers, etc, or whether each floor or area should have its own equipment. Sizes of equipment will have to be considered when planning storage for these items and some typical dimensions are shown below.

Powered domestic cleaning equipment

Cylinder and hand-held vacuum cleaners require a minimum space, when stacked, 700mm high and 300mm deep

Upright vacuum cleaners and polishers require a minimum space 1300mm high, 450mm deep and 600mm wide

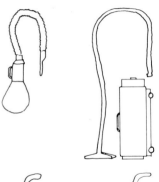

Small cleaning equipment

Buckets, dustpans and pails require a minimum space 300mm high and 300mm deep

Brooms, mops and ironing boards require a minimum space 1500mm high and 300mm deep

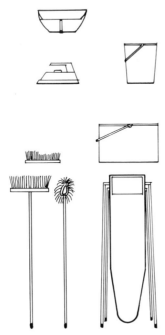

Commercial cleaning equipment

Trolley cleaners require a minimum space 1000mm high, 750mm deep and 1200mm wide

Polishers and large vacuum cleaners require a minimum space 1400mm high, 900mm deep and 500mm wide

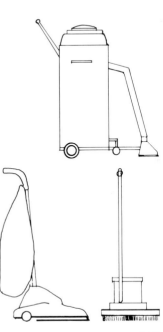

Cooking equipment and food preparation

A wide range of catering equipment is available and it is essential to choose the right equipment for the job in order to keep capital and running costs to a minimum. A detailed appraisal of the end product – the type of food to be served – will determine the equipment required. The basic choice is between convenience food, self-service food, and gourmet food, as discussed in Section 5.

Having listed the types of equipment required, a detailed study of the models produced by different manufacturers must be made before deciding on the type of fuel, flexibility and control needed. Look critically at the equipment: has the manufacturer given enough thought to ease of use, ease of cleaning, flexibility, coupling with other items of equipment and maintenance? All equipment must be easily cleaned and have no sharp edges to cut fingers or difficult corners that collect dirt and grease. Materials and finishes are important. Any gaps and voids must be completely sealed against dirt, animals and insects. Spaces below equipment should be accessible for easy cleaning.

Storage for vegetables and dry goods can be provided in the form of racks, shelving and trays, as necessary.

The quality and quantity of frozen foods used will determine whether or not a refrigerated cold room will be needed, or if a large deep freeze will be sufficient. Different types of food need to be stored at different temperatures: fresh meat at $1°C$, frozen meat at $-8°C$, wet fish at $0°C$, milk and dairy produce at 4 to $5°C$, and general cold room temperature should be 4 to $5°C$. Fish is the major problem and if large quantities are required this must be kept in a separate storage cabinet. Chest type deep freezers are more efficient than cabinets but they take up more floor space and it is more difficult to find food in them. The amount of ice and ice cream used will determine whether or not separate conservators and ice makers should be provided in addition to a freezer.

Double sinks are desirable for soaking and cleaning vegetables and other food before cooking. Surfaces for preparing food must be easily cleaned and stainless steel is an excellent material. A chopping surface, often in the form of a portable and renewable chopping block, will also be needed.

The amount of equipment required for preparing meat will depend on the scale of the establishment. It can include hand tools or mechanical meat saws, mincing machines, sausage machines, steak tenderisers and slicing machines.

Weighing and mixing equipment will be needed for pastry preparation. It is essential to choose equipment with the capacity to cope with peak demands.

The success of the kitchen will depend on the choice of the equipment in it. Cooking equipment can be fuelled by gas, electricity, oil or solid fuel. The choice here will depend on availability and price, which of course varies from time to time. There are three main types of oven: the conventional cooker is generally used in small establishments; larger hotels and restaurants often use the more traditional oven; and a more recent development is the forced convection oven. The traditional oven has the disadvantage of being large and it heats food almost entirely by convection. This means that the temperature is different in different parts of the oven and food has to be moved from one part to another. The forced convection oven is popular because it cooks food quickly, is flexible in use, cooks food evenly and can pre-heat frozen food. Microwave ovens, if used for the right purposes, are also good. They are primarily used for cooking food rapidly or reheating small, often individual portions of pre-cooked frozen foods. They make food appear less attractive as the radiation does not brown the food, but extra infra-red heating elements can be included to brown the food if this is required. Cooking times can be measured in seconds rather than minutes.

Pastry or baking ovens are unlikely to be necessary except in very large establishments.

Domestic saucepans are big enough for most hotels and restaurants and it is unlikely that the commercial boiling pans used in industrial and public catering will be needed.

Many hotels, restaurants and snack bars need facilities for quick frying of small portions and it is often better to have a bank of two friers from the point of view of flexibility.

Ease of use, maintenance and hygiene are important factors in the choice of kitchen equipment and the planning of cooking facilities

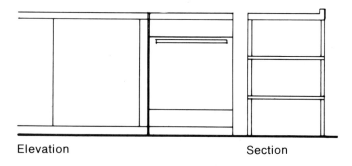

Elevation   Section

Kitchen surfaces should
not have sharp corners or
gaps that are too small to
be cleaned and joints
should be well sealed

The aim should be to produce food as and when it is required and to serve it immediately it is cooked. However, there will have to be some facilities for keeping cooked food and a hot cupboard can be used for this and for warming dishes. The top of the cupboard can incorporate a bain marie unit that will hold pans or containers of hot foods and gravies. Hot food and crockery should be stored at between 73–88°C to prevent the growth of bacteria, drying out, and damage to crockery. Some hot cupboards have double sides through which food can be passed.

The area for washing up should be well designed to cope with the return of crockery, cutlery, silver and glassware. There must be an adequately large receiving table with facilities for scraping off uneaten food, possibly with a commercial waste disposal unit. The washing up arrangements will vary depending on the through-put and washing can be done by hand, by large domestic type washing up machine, semi-automatic push-through type machine, or the automatic straight through dishwasher for very large establishments. Pans and cooking utensils are frequently washed by hand. Glass should be washed separately if possible from the main crockery and cutlery wash, in very clean water with a suitable detergent to avoid a streaky appearance. Mechanical glass washers are available and it is best to choose these after seeing them in operation. The success of the washing up operation will depend very much on having adequate space for loading and unloading machines or sinks easily.

Equipment for making and serving drinks and beverages will depend on the size of the establishment. Attractively designed coffee makers can be in full view, with the glass container itself used at the table. A hot water boiler may be needed for tea and other hot drinks and large models can be fitted with side urns for milk and coffee.

Careful thought should be given to how the various items of equipment will be installed and they should be chosen to be as compatible as possible. Provision must be made for joining them together if necessary and also for any changes of position in the future. Various materials and finishes are available but stainless steel predominates.

Grills provide only radiant heat and traditionally were appliances that were supplied with heat from below, by charcoal or gas, used for grilling meat in particular. Many new appliances are top fired. The combination of a top fired grill with a solid heated hearth has the advantage that food does not have to be turned. Grills heated from above are known as salamanders. Heated plate grillers are used in some snack bars and particularly in hamburger bars.

If a conventional cooking range or oven is used the top will be fitted with boiling plates, but if convection ovens and microwave ovens are used it will be necessary to consider independent boiling plates for use with saucepans and frying pans.

There is a choice of three main types of toaster, from the shelf type usually found in domestic cookers, the automatic, pop-up type and, for very large quantities, the rotary type with automatic delivery, which can produce very large quantities of toast. The salamander type of grill can also be used for toast making.

Mechanical services, heating and ventilation

The large hotel or motel will have a sophisticated system of heating and ventilation which will have to be designed by experts. Some alternative ideas are suggested below, but they are in no way intended to replace the advice of the consultant in this area who can produce a tailor-made solution. The suggestions for smaller schemes are also likely to require professional advice when it comes to detail design and installation.

Financial resources will dictate what type of scheme can be installed and it is essential to balance cost with actual needs in order to avoid overspending in some important areas.

There are a number of points that should be considered when thinking about a small-scale scheme:

1 The British climate does not make the use of air-conditioning essential and most guests will in any case want different conditions. A guest staying at a country hotel, for example, will want to control the heating and open the windows
2 Noise is often a problem with air-conditioning and ventilation systems. Low-cost installations work with high-velocity air in small ducts and are therefore noisier than the more expensive types, which are larger
3 All systems use fuel and economy in use is important

So far as the type of fuel is concerned, the initial step is to evaluate the capital costs of installation and the subsequent costs of running the system. Try to take availability and price of fuel in the future into account. In general terms, solid fuel requires considerable space for storage and is comparatively dirty in use. Oil fuels must also be stored and smell can be a problem in confined areas, but it is still a competitive fuel for large installations. Gas needs no storage and is very competitive for small installations, although the margin reduces with size. For small installations on a domestic scale the balanced flue type of boiler has the advantage of not needing a separate flue or additional air intake. Electricity is expensive but convenient. Solar heating is a possibility but is in the early stages of development and at present has a high capital cost compared with savings in running costs. The only way to arrive at running costs is to specify your requirements in detail and discuss them with the relevant authorities.

HEAT CONSERVATION

Exposed sites will increase heating costs, but modifying the contours of the site and planting trees and shrubs for shelter will help

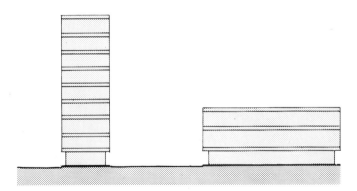

The shape of buildings is also important. Low buildings will, in general, have less heat loss and solar gain than a tall thin block

It is important to choose equipment that can be easily and economically maintained with the least possible disruption of the normal running of the hotel.

Individual room thermostats to control warm air or radiator valves in bedrooms are a good way of saving fuel as they can be turned down by staff when rooms are vacated.

There are eight primary choices of heating system, as follows:

1 Simple hot water radiators with manual valves or thermostats
2 Convectors with manual valves or thermostats
3 Warm air heating
4 Storage heaters
5 Underfloor heating
6 Ceiling heating
7 Individual air conditioning units for each room
8 Full air conditioning by central plant

The aim of any heating system is to provide a comfortable environment for the human body and different people's requirements will vary in this respect, depending on their age and how active they are. The quality of the environment and whether people feel comfortable will depend on the air temperature, the amount of radiant heat, the level of humidity and air movement, but it is generally accepted that a mercury thermometer is a sufficient guide. On this basis, room temperatures should be between 17–22°C while circulation areas can be lower, between 13–18°C. The system should be sufficiently flexible to enable some individual control of heating and ventilation for each area of the building.

The positioning of heating appliances and their controls should be considered to ensure that they do not detract from the visual appearance of the interior. Insufficient thought is often given to piping and to the noise produced by mechanical services. Heavy equipment, such as boilers, pumps, ventilation plant, etc, should be positioned to avoid affecting guests, remembering that noise can be transferred through pipes and ducts to other rooms.

Rising energy costs make it important for the designer to pay more attention both to control of the heating system and insulation of the building. Public

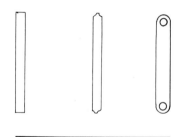

HEATING AND VENTILATION

Radiators
Flat panel
Panel single or double
Traditional steel
or cast iron

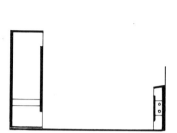

Convectors
Standard convectors can be wall or floor mounted
Skirting heating system
Existing large radiators can be converted to convectors with casing

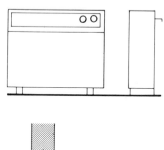

Electric heating
Night storage heaters

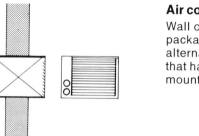

Air conditioning
Wall or window mounted package units are an alternative to large units that have to be floor mounted

buildings should have draughts lobbies to reduce heat loss and the size of windows should be limited and, if possible, double glazed. Temperature can be greatly affected by having excessively large south or west-facing windows where solar gain makes it difficult to keep the building adequately ventilated and cooled.

The hot water installation is frequently part of the heating system. There must be an adequate supply of hot water at peak periods and also adequate heating for towel rails etc during the period that the heating system as a whole is switched off. Towel rails on their own may not provide adequate heating for bathrooms and a separate radiator with an unheated towel rail may be more efficient.

The statutory authority should be consulted about storage requirements for cold water and the number of taps that can be taken from the rising main. It is obviously better for washbasins in hotels to be supplied from the rising main as they can therefore also supply drinking water. Baths and showers with mixer taps must be supplied from tanks to ensure an even pressure consistent with the hot water supply system and to avoid contamination of the mains. Pipe sizes will affect the water pressure and make mixer taps function badly. Where rooms are near the top of the building and the head of water is a problem it is possible to have a pumped supply of water to shower fittings, although this increases installation and running costs.

Careful consideration should be given to correct lay-out of the plumbing system to give easy access in case of blockages. Valves to isolate fittings for rewashering are well worth providing right at the start. Choice of materials depends not only on cost but also on durability and quietness in operation. Copper is a well tried material for piping and it lasts well and gives few problems. Stainless steel is more difficult to work with. Plastics are more vulnerable and can give rise to leaks; light materials are also often noisier in use. Cast iron can be used for soil and ventilation pipes if noise has to be reduced where pipes travel through bedrooms, for example.

So far as fittings are concerned, there is an infinite variety to choose from. Concussion taps, for example, switch off by a spring mechanism and can be infuriating to use, but they do save water. It is worth remembering that the streamlined design of some modern taps can, if taken to extremes, be difficult for elderly or young people to use because they find the smooth shape difficult to grip. Mixer taps can be thermostatically controlled.

119

Ventilation

The large, sophisticated air conditioning systems required for large hotels need expert design and are beyond the scope of this book. But ventilation can be as simple as an extractor fan. Some general points to consider when specifying equipment are:

1 The number of air changes required in rooms in a given time
2 The need for rapid response, which can be a big problem in hotels, restaurants and bars where numbers of guests fluctuate widely
3 Position of extractors which should not be such as to cause discomfort from the point of view of draughts or noise
4 Individual air conditioning units can be wall or window mounted and are about the size of a television set. They can be useful for small rooms but it is worth seeing them in operation before buying to assess the noise level and efficiency of different designs
5 Large, freestanding air conditioning units are quite expensive to run but may be the only answer where one public room needs air conditioning and a total installation is too expensive

Air extraction without air conditioning can be used in various parts of the building but it is most frequently found in kitchens, toilets, bathrooms and bars. The following points may be useful:

1 For toilets and bathrooms a number of individual units have been produced in response to the considerable demand for ventilation of internal spaces. These are often in the form of a simple mechanical ventilator operated by the light switch with a delay mechanism that provides adequate extraction after the room is vacated. The loo vent is connected to the outside by a simple duct
2 Adequate ventilation is essential for the main cooking area in kitchens. Intensive use can result in a fire hazard from the build-up of grease. It is important to incorporate adequate grease filters that can be easily removed for cleaning. These should be at the point of extract and close to cooking appliances. Canopies over cooking areas should be simple and designed for ease of cleaning. Any light fittings positioned within

them should be waterproof to minimise danger due to condensation and to help with cleaning. The discharge from extractors should be carefully sited to avoid inconvenience to other parts of the building or to neighbours
3 In bars, the main problem of heat build-up is often found near the counter and this is therefore the best place to site extractors if a suitable canopy can be provided. Noise must be taken into consideration and individual extractor fans with variable speeds have an advantage in that they enable staff to reduce air movement when few people are using the room so as to keep background noise to a minimum. High-speed fans produce higher velocity air movement and therefore more noise and a low fan operating at slow speed will generally give better results

Insulation

It is impossible to consider heating and ventilation adequately without taking insulation into account. In addition to saving costs, insulation improves the comfort of a building by minimising temperature changes within the total complex and even within each room. Insulation also has the advantage of reducing condensation, which can be an acute problem in densely populated spaces. Points to consider, related to the various parts of the building, are as follows:

1 The construction of the floor at ground level can be a large source of heat loss – maybe as much as one sixth of the total loss in a building. Ventilation under suspended floors is essential to reduce the risk of decay, so solid floors are warmer than suspended timber ones. Damp must be avoided as moisture is a good conductor of heat. The surface treatment of the floor will have an effect on heat loss and can give a psychological feeling of warmth in the room

INSULATION

Heat insulation

75mm glass fibre quilt laid over joists

Vermiculite fill between joists

Sealing strips for
doors and windows

Nylon brush seal

Plastic foam strip

Metal or plastic
draught excluding strip

Double doors with
draught lobby

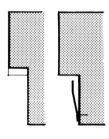

Sealed double glazing units

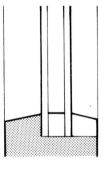

Sound insulation

Double windows with
wide gap between
Heavy materials such as
concrete, brick or sand

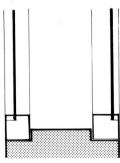

2 New buildings should be constructed with cavity walls to give maximum insulation and minimum moisture transfer from the exterior to the inside. Filling the cavity with foam or mineral wool should be considered, but this can produce problems if the cavity is bridged and building regulation approval is necessary. It is preferable to increase the insulation value of the inner skin and maintain a sealed cavity. Surface treatments applied to inner walls can improve insulation but the fire officer must be consulted to ensure that spread of flame classifications are maintained

3 The size of windows is a critical factor in reducing the problem of heat loss and double glazing offers the advantage of cutting down heat losses and reducing condensation. Solar gain must not be overlooked and, if large expanses of glass are used, it is better to arrange for the windows to be shaded from outside. If this is not possible then reflective surfaces should be considered in the form of venetian blinds or heat-reflecting nets

4 Roofs are also a major source of heat loss. Pitched roofs can be easily insulated with a 75mm thick layer of glass fibre or mineral fill. Good insulation is also essential for flat roofs, but this may be more difficult

Confusion frequently arises between materials for sound and heat insulation, and the two are not the same thing. Sound insulation is provided by heavy materials. Brick, concrete, plaster and lead are all good sound insulators. Light materials, in the form of acoustic tiles and materials, have little value other than reducing reverberation in a space and thus improving the quality of sound in it. They do not prevent sound passing through to other areas. In addition to providing sound insulation it may be necessary to isolate noisy machinery by using sound insulating pads or floating structures to prevent structure-borne sounds penetrating other parts of the building.

Heat insulating materials are usually light in weight and cellular in structure. Materials most extensively used in buildings are expanded polystyrene, glass fibre, fibreboard, vermiculite, mineral wool and form plastics. Double glazing incorporating a cavity between two sheets of glass can improve both heat and sound insulation of windows.

121

Fire prevention

Fire is an ever-present hazard in hotels and restaurants and its prevention, detection and extinction must be carefully considered. There are three stages: assessing the hazard of fire; insuring the building; and complying with the requirements of the Building Regulations and the fire officer.

Designing a building so as to take into consideration all the problems related to fire prevention is a complex business. Among the points to consider are:

1 Free access for fire appliances to all parts of the building

2 Control of fire spread between buildings and from buildings outside the site itself

3 Control of fire spread within the building. Here the hazards may be difficult to see; they range from the surface spread of fire to hidden channels in the form of ducts and voids, chutes and suspended ceilings. It is essential that fire division walls are continued through ducts and voids

4 Fire exits and escape routes must be assessed with the fire officer and clearly signposted

5 Fire appliances and equipment fall into three groups: detection, warning and extinguishing. The method to be adopted for detection and warning must be agreed with the fire officer in advance and can range from hand-bells to an electrically operated warning system with points throughout the building, which is to be preferred. Automatic systems rely on sensitive detector heads connected to indicator boards and warning devices. They can also be monitored in a central alarm office or fire brigade headquarters. All alarm systems must be tested regularly and all members of staff must be made aware of their responsibilities in case of fire

6 Fire-fighting equipment must also be discussed with the fire officer who will be able to give expert advice on anything from hose reels to automatic sprinklers, portable extinguishers and buckets

7 If the fire brigade is a long way from the building the detection system must be even quicker and more responsive. It may be necessary to consider having a fully automatic system

8 The integration of fire protection equipment into

FIRE EQUIPMENT

Sprinkler system to provide overall automatic fire extinguishment

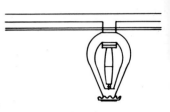

Automatic detection and warning system with smoke/heat detector, bell and indicators

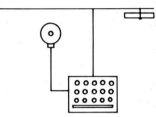

Hose reel

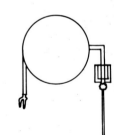

Extinguishers
Hand-held and trolley mounted
Fire buckets

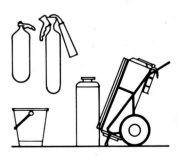

FIRE RESISTANT DOORS

One-hour fire resistant door 60/60

25mm rebate in solid frame
Three broad flap hinges
Maximum 0.5 sq metres
6mm wired glass
Self closing (not
rising butts)

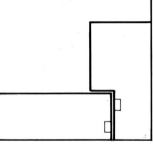

Half-hour fire resistant door 30/30

25mm rebate in solid frame
or screwed and glued
to lining
Three hinges
Maximum 1.2 sq metres 6mm
wired glass
Self closing (not
rising butts)

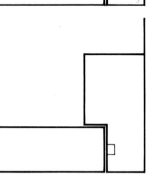

Half-hour fire check door 30/20

25mm rebate in solid or
screwed and glued frame
Two hinges
Maximum 1.2 sq metres
6mm wired glass

In certain cases it may be
possible to negotiate
suitable treatment for
existing doors in listed
buildings, such as an
asbestos lining and a
planted stop to increase
rebate to 25mm with an
intumescent strip in
the frame

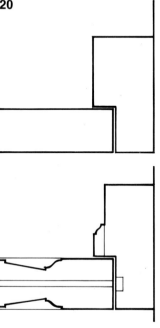

Recess for hose reel and
extinguishers with nearby
alarm bell, avoiding
obstruction and
improving appearance

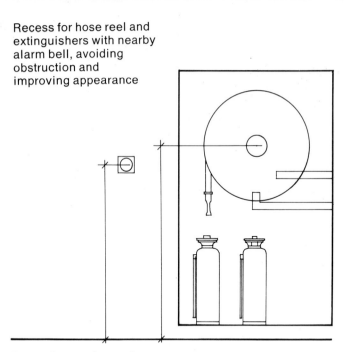

Detection and warning system

Bells must be audible
throughout the building
and connected to both
mains and emergency
power supply.

An alarm signal to the fire
brigade can be arranged

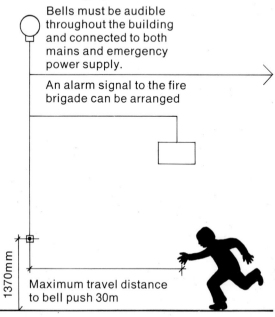

1370mm

Maximum travel distance
to bell push 30m

the overall design of the building must be considered, as badly sited equipment and signs can mar an otherwise satisfactory scheme

9 The question of the fire resistance of the buildings should be discussed with the building control officer and the fire officer in the light of the building regulations and relevant British Standards. The materials and form of construction used will have to be considered and will also be of interest to the insurers of the building, whose premiums can be affected by these points

10 Means of escape are most important. The principle that must be followed is that every person in the building must be able to find a safe way to a safe area outside. Escape routes must be planned to cope with an outbreak of fire in the same room by providing a horizontal route at the same level as the outbreak and also a separate, vertical route that can still be used when there is a fire at a lower level

11 Fire doors are a vital part of the escape system but they can themselves be sources of danger due to misuse, particularly in hotels and restaurants where it may be difficult to manoeuvre through them with trays etc and there is the chance of staff wedging the doors open. It may be preferable to discuss the matter with the fire officer and spend rather more on fitting smoke or heat detectors connected to magnetic door holders that will shut the doors automatically in case of fire

12 Emergency lighting must be provided for all means of escape and this, together with associated signposting, will have to be carefully designed to match the interior

The following notes may be of use in selecting materials to minimise fire risks. They are taken from *Surface finishes of walls and ceilings*, the appendix to *Guides to the Fire Precautions Act 1971, Hotels and Boarding Houses*, published by HMSO. This is a section that may change, however, and it is advisable to check the latest position with the fire officer.

A Inorganic group. This includes brickwork, blockwork, concrete, plasterboard, ceramic tiles, plaster finishes (including rendering on wood or metal laths) and asbestos boards

B Cellulosic group (untreated). This includes timber, hardboard, particleboard or chipboard and blockboard. These materials are acceptable in small rooms with a floor area not exceeding 3·7 square metres. They are also acceptable in small areas of larger rooms provided that they do not exceed either half the floor area or 18 square metres. They are not acceptable on escape routes such as staircases, corridors or entrance halls

C Cellulosic group (flame retardant treated). Treated materials in group B are acceptable in all rooms, provided that evidence of suitable treatment is available. They are not, however, acceptable on escape routes

D Woodwool slab. Acceptable in all locations

E Plastics (thermosetting). These materials, which are usually decorative laminates, are acceptable as for group B unless they can be shown to be of flame retardant grade, in which case acceptability will be as for group C

F Plastics (thermoplastic). These materials include expanded polystyrene wall and ceiling lining materials. They are acceptable on inorganic surfaces in thicknesses not exceeding 5mm on walls and 12mm on ceilings, provided they are not finished in gloss paint, in the same locations as for group B. Expanded polystyrene that has been gloss painted is not permitted and must be removed

G Thin vinyl and paper coverings (other than heavy flock wallpaper). These are acceptable in all locations if they cover inorganic surfaces

H Heavy flock wallpapers. These are acceptable as for group B unless they can be shown to be of flame retardant grade, in which case acceptability will be as for group C

There are now many types of flame retardant fabric on the market and these cost very little more than untreated ones. The retardant ingredient is usually incorporated when the fabric is being dyed, which means that little extra cost is added. Man-made fibres are more difficult to treat, but they can be coated, or the materials used can be made inherently flame retardant. Cleaning treated fabrics can remove the retardant material, but most cleaning firms provide a re-treatment service.

Security

The security of hotels and restaurants provides a major challenge to the designer. Correct basic planning of the building will help considerably in its ease of running and subsequent security. There are four basic considerations:

1 Providing a plan form that makes it difficult for staff and guests to come and go unobserved, with a strategically positioned reception area. This will help considerably in monitoring the movement of guests and differentiating those who are visiting for a short period from the long-term guests
2 Ensuring security for the reception desk and, in the case of hotels, the security of the room key system
3 Ensuring the security of personal valuables
4 Ensuring the security of the property itself and its contents and equipment

Consult and take the advice of the police and the insurance company at an early stage and build on the experience of those who have been involved with this type of problem. The developments of the past few years have made it even more necessary in many instances to take into consideration the unpleasant prospect of a lunatic fringe using bombs. The size of the problem will increase with the size of the establishment. In small hotels and restaurants every member of the staff is known, as are many of the customers, but more and more sophisticated checks will be needed as numbers of staff and guests increase and management becomes more remote from both groups.

Strategic siting of the reception area will help considerably in the subtle control of guest movement. Unobstructed views of staircases are essential from this point and staff who help guests should be encouraged to monitor their movement as much as possible for the safety of all concerned.

Staff must be controlled as well, particularly in large establishments, and this also applies to stock of all kinds. Again, correct fundamental planning of the building will reduce problems to a minimum.

Careful siting of the reception desk will not only help in controlling the movement of guests and staff, but it will also make the receptionist and cashier less vulnerable. The more visible everything is, the more difficult a thief will find it to operate.

The room key system must be effective, with locks that are difficult to tamper with. There should be adequate space in pigeon holes next to keys for messages, passports and other documents belonging to guests to be kept and returned to them easily.

The degree of sophistication necessary for security of guests' valuables will depend on the scale of the hotel and the wealth of its clientele. Guests who must have secure storage for their personal possessions will expect the management to provide a safe deposit box in the reception area. Any doubts about the trustworthiness of staff can be resolved by the use of either two keys or a key on a card, one being kept by the guest, so that the safe deposit can only be opened in their presence. Less sophisticated systems can also be employed in which less valuable articles are put in a single safe in the reception area.

The management's concern extends to personal belongings that are not put into the care of the hotel, and the security of the bedroom locking system is therefore important. Doors should be self-locking so that guests cannot forget to lock them when they go out, with a master key for the use of staff. In restaurants and other public areas of the building, coats should either by deposited in the care of staff or hung on coat stands that are strategically placed to enable guests to keep an eye on them.

In terms of the security of the property itself and its contents, controls at staff entrances and the reception area are just as important as proper locks on doors and windows. Remember that large sheets of glass give greater protection than small ones, making illegal entry difficult because a large area of glass must be broken first. Within the building certain areas will require additional security, including wine, spirit and beer stores and bars. The designer should consider the aesthetic appearance of shutter grilles at the bar, the design of locks, and the appearance of doors and windows to enable adequate security standards to be achieved throughout the building together with good looks and ease of operation.

Alarm systems are unlikely to be needed for all parts of the building but in the case of personal security safes, the wine and spirit areas and any valuable fittings, such as very expensive works of art, it may be necessary to take the precaution of having an alarm system. This can be in the form of an audible alarm intended to attract the attention of passers-by but, unfortunately, the number of alarm bells that tend to ring in cities means that people often ignore the noise and it may be better to have a direct connection with the police station.

Fire escape routes are a potential security risk and panic bolts can easily be slipped by an accomplice inside the building to allow strangers into the building. Constant inspection is the only answer here.

Communications systems

No attempt is made in this section to be comprehensive. The scale of the building will indicate the magnitude of the problem: small establishments will need little more than a telephone but as the size increases the amount of equipment involved can become staggering, and will in the end result in the need for expert advice. This section therefore simply suggests some of the areas in which action will have to be taken. It is essential to avoid the disastrous effect of surface wiring associated with a proliferation of communications equipment. Conduits should be built in from the start and it is better to over-specify at the beginning as the demand for more and more visual aids is likely to increase in the future. Among the points to consider are the following:

1 Telephone. Post Office staff will advise on the number of different systems available. It is essential to give them a clear brief and to think out the real requirements of the system to enable the best advice to be given by engineers. Questions to ask are: is the telephone required for more than reception and strategic staff control points? Is the telephone to be connected to each bedroom and, if so, will a metering device for recording calls and billing guests be needed? Is a public telephone required?

2 Call systems. Will an independent paging system be needed to call guests? This can be very disturbing but may be the only solution in large buildings. An alternative system for calling guests may be provided by the use of an internal phone system. In large buildings some form of staff paging will be needed. This can be provided successfully by a bleep system with pocket receivers for staff and this will avoid a loudspeaker system distracting the guests

3 Assembly rooms, banqueting and conference areas will need good public address systems. A fundamental appraisal of needs is essential so that a comprehensive brief can be given to the outside expert. The types of equipment that may be needed include: dimmer controls on lights; microphones and loudspeakers; moveable telephones; overhead projectors; projection facilities for slides and films; translation facilities with consoles and headsets; and film screens, blackboards and display boards. A sophisticated system will certainly need expert planning and installation

4 Radio and television. A decision should be made at an early stage on the relative costs of rented and bought equipment. It is worth noting that radios can be used for fire alarm purposes. The cost of maintaining the equipment, running it and licensing it must be taken into account

5 Background music. Considerable research has been undertaken by commercial companies that sell 'canned' music. The intention is to heighten the customers' mood and the research has aimed at identifying the effect needed at different times. The surveys extend to the effect that music has on guests' feelings, conditioning them for eating, relaxing and general comfort in the case of hotels and restaurants. Introducing canned music into a building is a fundamental design decision. The eye is not the only sense and the effect of music must be considered in depth. It is, of course, resented by many guests.

8 LEGISLATION AND REGULATIONS

The law affecting buildings in general, and hotels, restaurants and pubs in particular, is a vast subject in its own right. The proliferation of legislation has resulted from successive reactions of government to different pressures, and the process is cumulative since very few pieces of old legislation affecting buildings are rescinded when new Acts are passed. The following Acts and statutes are some of the major ones affecting the planning and management of hotels, restaurants and pubs in England and Wales.

Licensing Act 1964
Licences must be obtained for places of public entertainment, such as hotels, restaurants and bars for music, dancing, showing films and dispensing liquor. The Licensing Act will affect the great majority of hotels and restaurants, since it is an offence to sell drink without a licence. When planning a hotel or restaurant the first step is to decide on the type of licence that is required, which can vary from a simple table licence covering the consumption of drinks with food to a full publican's licence. The attitudes of the local licensing justices to the idea should be ascertained; the Act enables local justices to grant a provisional licence in respect of buildings not yet constructed. Plans will have to be drawn up and deposited, and the services of an architect with experience of the field will help. It is important, however, to allow for planning alterations to the design required by the justices.

Licensed premises can be used at any time; the law only controls the hours during which liquor can be sold. This can give rise to confusion. It follows that bars in multi-function areas must be able to be closed to the public by lockable shutters or divisions. These should fit in with the general design of the building. The justices will consult the police on the suitability of the design of the building for the sale of liquor, so it is advisable to get the reaction of the police to the plans before making a formal application for the licence. The fire officer will also be consulted by the justices. However, fire requirements are also covered by the Building Regulations and the Fire Precautions Act, which extend the liability of the owner beyond the requirements of the licence.

Town and Country Planning Act 1971
as amended by the *Town and Country Planning* (Amendment) *Act 1972*
as amended by the *Town and Country Amenities Act 1974*
Approval is required under these Acts for any new building, for external alterations to a building in the form of an extension, for other changes to the external envelope of a building, and for change of use. Consultation with the local planning authority at an early stage is essential, and vehicular access and car parking provisions are an important factor in the case of hotels and restaurants. Special provisions have to be made for demolition or alterations to Listed Buildings and buildings in Conservation Areas, about which the local authority can advise.

Building Regulations 1976
The building regulations affect the design and construction of new buildings, and alterations to existing ones, in England and Wales, but excluding London, which is covered by the London Building Acts. They cover the construction of buildings and the materials to be used in them; the space surrounding buildings; lighting, ventilation and the dimensions of habitable rooms; the height of buildings and chimneys; works, services and fittings, including drainage, sanitation, cesspools, septic tanks and private sewers, heating and cooking appliances, water supply and ash pits; structural fire precautions; and thermal and sound insulation and structural stability. Plans must be submitted to the local authority for Building Regulations approval. The building control office, which is usually part of the city or district engineer's department, will provide the necessary forms and advice.

London Building Act 1930
as amended by *London Building Act 1935*
as amended by *London Building Act (Amendments) Act 1939*
These Acts govern building in London, specifically the old London County Council area, including party structures. They affect all building in the central London area, which is under the control of the District Surveyor, a statutory officer peculiar to London with wide powers and responsibilities. Once again, early consultation is recommended. Party structures include the rights of adjoining owners of walls and fences.

GLC London Building Acts 1930–39 Constructional Bye-laws
GLC London Building Acts (Amendments) Act 1939 Section 20
GLC London Building (Constructional) Bye-laws 1972
GLC Places of Public Entertainment Technical Regulations
All these regulations affect building in London. Licences must be obtained for places of public entertainment.

Public Health Acts (Amendment) Act 1890
as amended by *Public Health (London) Act 1936*
as amended under *Section 147 of London Government Act 1938 and 1963*
as amended by *Public Health Act 1961*
GLC Drainage Bye-laws (London) arising out of the *Public Health Act 1936*
All these contain regulations governing construction, amenities, waste disposal etc. For buildings outside London, local district council regulations will apply. There are numerous requirements to ensure hygiene, drainage, sewerage, toilet accommodation, water supply, refuse removal and exits and entrances for public buildings.

Community Land Act 1975
This act provides for the progressive municipal ownership of all land. In April 1976 local authorities were given power to acquire development land under this Act. Small projects, conversions, changes of use and land in charity ownership are generally exempt. The object is to enable the community as a whole to control the development of land according to public needs and priorities, and to see that the community benefits from the increased land values that result. Small hotels, restaurants and commercial buildings will be exempt

where their gross floor area is under 1000 square metres and where rebuilding or enlargement of an existing building does not increase the original gross floor area by more than 10 per cent.

Development Land Tax Act 1976
This provides for a tax on the increased value of land arising out of its development.

Highways Act 1959
as amended by *Highways (Miscellaneous Provisions) Act 1961*
as amended by *Highways Act 1971*
Private Street Work Act 1961
These cover the creation of highways, tunnels, new streets, private roads and the diversion or closure of roads.

Fire Services Act 1947
Fire Precautions Act 1971
The later piece of legislation was designed to cover the upgrading of existing buildings, leaving new buildings under the control of the Building Regulations. Hotels and boarding houses are the first to be designated under the Act. There are three main items: escape route layout; fire resisting construction; and equipment for warning, fire fighting, emergency lighting and pressurisation.

The shape of the building will affect the criteria for designing escape routes, and a long low building clearly has fewer problems than the cube or tall one. It is possible to make all shapes reasonably safe, however, although the shape will determine how sophisticated the details must be.

The contents of hotels are affected by the Act, particularly in communal spaces, and the usefulness of escape routes must not be reduced in operation. People using hotels are divided into two groups under the Act: staff and guests. The staff are responsible for maintaining and being familiar with fire equipment, warning systems and groups. Staff should be regularly trained and tested, which is most important when staff turnover is high or casual or part-time staff are used. Fire alarms must be loud enough to awaken sleeping guests and be at least 5dBa louder than any other signal. Visual alarms can be used in addition to audible ones and safe exists from bedrooms must be provided. The problem with non-sleeping guests is to provide enough escape routes for large numbers of people. The Act covers escape route geometry, shape and length.

The construction of old hotels and restaurants can be brought up to standard by applying lining and board materials to the structure and by using cavity barriers and intumescent materials (ones that expand with heat to fill cavities or seal doors).

The section of the Act on warning devices starts from the premise that people are more important than goods. When a fire occurs, people must be warned in time to escape safely, which raises two considerations: fire detection and fire warning. There are two main types of detector for hotels, heat and smoke. In tall buildings it may be necessary to have the detectors linked directly to the fire control system of sprinklers. Regular maintenance of equipment is essential to ensure a reliable system.

Once a fire has been detected the alarm must be given very clearly. Call points must be positioned strategically along escape routes and they must not be further apart than 16 metres. There are automatic systems available that detect fire and provide an alarm signal by bells, sirens, warble-tone devices, klaxons, flashing lights or vibrators. In large hotels a direct line to a central control point, and in some cases to the local fire brigade, is a great advantage. Detectors and alarms should preferably not be run off the mains supply, but off a separate emergency supply.

Hotels are considered to be high life-risk premises where every outbreak of fire could be a threat to occupants. Adequate fire-fighting facilities must be available in the form of extinguishers, hose reels and buckets, positioned in agreement with the fire prevention officer, who is responsible for issuing a Fire Certificate on completion of a new building. This certificate also requires that staff will be regularly trained in fire drill.

Emergency lighting provision is another important part of the Act and reference should be made to BS 5266 Emergency Lighting of Premises, Part 1 of which covers premises other than cinemas and certain other specified premises used for entertainment. Lighting must indicate fire escape routes clearly and unambiguously; allow safe movement along such routes

and through exits; ensure that fire alarm call points and fire-fighting equipment can be readily located; and give clear signs of escape routes and exits.

Petroleum Consolidation Act 1928
Petroleum Spirit Motor Vehicles (Regulations) Act 1929
These are licensing regulations governing carparks where cars or petrol are involved. The second Act is concerned with smaller premises containing less than 12 cars or 60 gallons of petrol.

Chronically Sick and Disabled Persons Act 1970
This Act contains regulations governing the provision of special facilities for the disabled, and is therefore important in public buildings generally.

Offices, Shops and Railway Premises Act 1963
Factories Act 1961
The Offices, Shops and Railway Premises Act is an extension of the Factories Act and covers buildings that were exempt under the earlier legislation. Aspects covered include fire precautions, lighting, ventilation, heating, space and sanitary accommodation.

Clean Air Act 1956
as amended by *Clean Air Act 1968*
As their name suggests, these contain regulations governing air pollution.

Rights of Light Act 1959
Regulations governing rights to natural light, which may be affected by new building.

Private Places of Entertainment (Licensing) Act 1967
Betting, Gaming and Lotteries Act 1963
Home Counties (Music and Dancing) Licensing Act 1926
Cinematograph Act 1909 and 1952
These provide for the licensing of various activities other than the sale of liquor.

Development of Tourism Act 1969
This Act provides for financial assistance, by way of grant and/or loan, for certain classes of projects for tourist facilities.

Food and Hygiene Regulations 1970
The regulations cover catering businesses in addition to a number of other types of operation. As the name im-

plies, their main objective is hygiene. Part two of the regulations states that food must not be prepared or sold in insanitary places, gives details of cleanliness of equipment, and makes restrictions on the preparation and packing of food on domestic premises. Part three sets out requirements for the handling of food to protect it from contamination, including the need for special clothing, the transport and wrapping of food, and the exclusion of people suffering from certain infections. Part four concerns food premises, including drainage systems, water supply and sanitation, including the provision of hand basins, first aid materials and clothing storage. Other requirements cover lighting, ventilation, and general cleanliness and maintenance, together with the permitted temperature at which certain foods are to be kept. Part five sets out administrative provisions. The appropriate authority for the administration of the regulations is the local authority.

These are important regulations so far as hotels and restaurants are concerned and most establishments will clearly try to do better than the regulations require. There is an appeal procedure, but an offence against the regulations will, of course, not be good publicity for the establishment.

Health and Safety at Work Act 1974

This relatively recent legislation aims to provide a framework within which high standards of health and safety can be provided in all places of employment and, in addition, for the general public. It is in four parts: Part 1 relates to health and safety in relation to work; Part 2 relates to the Employment Medical Advisory Service; Part 3 amends the law relating to the Building Regulations; and Part 4 contains a number of miscellaneous and general provisions.

The Act is an enabling measure superimposed over the existing health and safety legislation, covering practically all people at work and also the protection of the public where they may be affected by the activities of people at work. It says that it is the duty of the employer to safeguard so far as is reasonably practical the health, safety and welfare of the people who work for him or come into contact with his premises. It is a statutory requirement for employers to prepare a written statement of their general policy, organisation and arrangements for health and safety at work, to keep it up to date by revisions, and to bring the statement to the notice of his employees. It is also the employer's duty to provide any necessary information and training in safe practices, including all the equipment and information required by the Fire Precautions Act. The Act covers responsibilities of self-employed persons, where a duty similar to that of employers exists in that they must avoid danger or risk to the health of other people and themselves.

Employees have a duty under the Act to take reasonable care to avoid injury to themselves or to others in their work and to co-operate with employers and others in meeting statutory requirements. The Act also requires employees not to interfere with or misuse anything provided to protect their health, safety or welfare in compliance with the Act.

Enforcement of the Act is delegated to local authorities, who can issue prohibition notices and prosecute any persons contravening a statutory provision. The maximum fine on summary conviction for most offences will be £400; there is no limit to the fine on contravention on indictment. Imprisonment for up to two years can be imposed for certain offences.

It is essential to be familiar with the requirements of this Act and, if in doubt about them, to consult the local factory inspector. It is advisable to keep an accident book, with details of the date, time, and brief particulars of any accidents. It is a criminal offence to contravene the Act and therefore no insurance cover can be provided.

9 SOURCES OF FURTHER INFORMATION

Information services

British Standards Institution, 2 Park Street, London W1A 2BS

Building Centres
26 Store Street, London WC1E 7BT
Broad Street, Birmingham BL 2DB
Colston Avenue, The Centre, Bristol BS1 4TW
15–16 Trumpington Street, Cambridge CB2 1QD
17 Lower Baggot Street, Dublin 2
Hope Street, Liverpool L1 9BR
113–115 Portland Street, Manchester M1 6FB
4 Arthur Place, Belfast BT1 4HJ
Mansfield Road, Nottingham NG1 3FE
6 Newton Terrace, Glasgow G3 7PF
18–20 Cumberland Place, Southampton SO1 2BD

National Building Research Establishment
Building Research Station,
Garston, Watford WD2 7JR

Design Council, The Design Centre
28 Haymarket, London SW1Y 4SU
and the Scottish Design Centre
72 St Vincent Street, Glasgow G2 5TN

HMSO (Stationery Office)
49 High Holborn, London WC1 6HB

National Building Specification
66 Portland Place, London W1N 4AD

RIBA Services Ltd,
66 Portland Place, London W1N 4AD

Professional services

Royal Institute of British Architects
66 Portland Place, London W1N 4AD

Institute of Landscape Architects
Nash House, 12 Carlton Terrace, London SW1

Royal Institute of Chartered Surveyors
12 Great George Street, London SW1

Chartered Auctioneers and Estate Agents Institute
29 Lincolns Inn Fields, London WC2

Association of Consulting Engineers
Abbey House, 2 Victoria Street, London SW1H 0LH

Institute of Structural Engineers
11 Upper Belgrave Street, London SW1 8BH

Royal Town Planning Institute
26 Portland Place, London W1N 4BE

Society of Industrial Artists and Designers
12 Carlton House Terrace, London SW1

Historic Buildings Council
25 Saville Row, London W1
21 Hill Street, Edinburgh
Summit House, Windsor Place, Cardiff CF 3BQ

The Institute of Chartered Accountants
Chartered Accountants Hall
Moorgate Place, London EC2R 6EQ

The Law Society, 29–37 Red Lion Street, London WC1

Association of Insurance Brokers
Craven House, Kingsway, London WC2 6PF

Royal Fine Art Commission
2 Carlton Gardens, London SW1Y 5AA

Ancient Monuments Board for England
Sanctuary Buildings, Great Smith Street, London SW1

Trade Associations and other organisations

Associated Master Plumbers and Domestic Engineers
Longwood, Kenley, Surrey

Association of Flooring Contractors
47 Great Russell Street, London WC1B 3PA

Brick Development Association
19 Grafton Street, London W1X 3LE

British Ceramic Tile Council
Federation House, Stoke-on-Trent, Staffs ST4 2RU

British Colour Council
21B Goodge Street, London W1P 2BN

British Plastics Federation Limited
47 Piccadilly, London W1V 0DN

British Linoleum Association
125 Queens Road, Brighton, Sussex BN1 3YW

British Woodwork Manufacturers Association
26 Store Street, London WC1E 7BT

Cement and Concrete Association
52 Grosvenor Gardens, London SW1W 0AQ

Contract Flooring Association Limited
23 Chippenham Mews, London W9 2AN

Copper Development Association
Orchard House, Mutton Lane, Potters Bar, Herts

Electrical Contractors Association
55 Catherine Place, London W2 4HY

Electricity Council Marketing Department
30 Millbank, London SW1 4PRD

Expanded Polystyrene Product Manufacturers
Association
16 Bolton Street, London W1Y 8HX

Federation of Master Builders
33 John Street, London W2 4HY

Federation of Stone Industries
Alderman House, 37 Soho Square, London W1V 6AT

Fibre Board Federation
Audley House, 9 Margaret Street, London W1N 7LF

Fibre Building Board Development Organisation
Limited
Buckingham House, 6–7 Buckingham Street,
London WC2N 6BZ

Fire Extinguishing Trades Association, The Secretary,
'Cairo', 74 Exmoor Drive, Worthing, Sussex BN13 2PJ

British Gas Corporation
59 Bryanston Street, London W1A 2AZ

Glazed and Floor Tile Association, Federation House,
Station Road, Stoke-on-Trent, Staffs ST4 2RU

Gypsum Products Development Association
15–17 Marylebone Road, London NW1 5JE

Heating and Ventilating Contractors Association
Coastal Chambers, 172 Buckingham Palace Road,
London SW1W 9TD

Incorporated Institute of British Decorators
and Interior Designers
162 Derby Road, Stapleford, Nottingham

Institute of Building
Englemere, Kings Ride, Ascot, Berks SL5

Institute of Plumbing
Scottish Mutual House, North Street, Hornchurch,
Essex

Insulation Glazing Association
6 Mount Row, London W1Y 6DY

Lead Development Association
34 Berkeley Square, London W1X 6AJ

Lighting Industry Federation
25 Bedford Square, London WC1 3HH

London Association of Master Decorators
37 Soho Square, London W1V 6AT

Mastic Asphalt Council and Employers Federation
24 Grosvenor Gardens, London SW1W 0DH

Metal Window Federation of Great Britain
26 Store Street, London WC1 7BS

National Federation of Building Trades
6 Fitzroy Place, Glasgow C3

National Federation of Building Trades Employers
82 New Cavendish Street, London W1M 8AD

National Federation of Demolition Contractors
2 Bankart Avenue, Leicester

National Federation of Master Painters
and Decorators of England and Wales
37 Soho Square, London W1V 6AT

National Federation of Plastering Contractors
82 New Cavendish Street, London W1M 8AD

National Federation of Terrazzo/Mosaic Specialists
City Wall House, 14/18 Finsbury Square,
London EC2Y 9AQ

National Heating Consultancy
188 Albany Street, London NW1 4AP

National Inspection Council for
Electrical Installation Contracting
93 Albert Embankment, London SE1 7PB

National Inspection Council for
Electrical Installation Contracting
1 Charing Cross, London SW1

Registered Plumbers Association
Scottish Mutual House, Hornchurch, Essex

Royal Society of Health
13 Grosvenor Place, London SW1 7EN

Structural Insulation Association
City Wall House, 14/18 Finsbury Street,
London EC2Y 9AQ

Timber Research and Development Association
The Building Centre, 26 Store Street,
London WC1E 7BT

Zinc Development Association
34 Berkeley Square, London W1X 6AJ

Bibliography

Architects' Journal (ed)	*Principles of hotel design*	Architectural Press, London, 1970
Bean, W. J.	*Trees and shrubs hardy in the British Isles (2 vols)*	John Murray, London, 1973
Boisot Waters Cohen Partnership (ed)	*The Community Land Act Explained*	
Doswell, R.	*Towards an integrated approach to hotel planning*	New University Education, London, 1970
Home Office	*Guide to the Fire Precautions Act 1971, 1 Hotels and boarding-houses*	HMSO, London, 1972
IES	*Code of recommendations for good interior lighting*	Illuminating Engineering Society, London, 1968
Lawson, F. R.	*Principles of catering design*	Architectural Press, London, 1973
Lawson, F. R.	*Hotels, motels and condominiums*	Architectural Press, London, 1976
Lawson, F. R.	*Restaurant planning and design*	Architectural Press, London, 1973
Lundberg, D. E.	*The hotel and restaurant business*	Cahners, Boston Mass, 1971
Strank, R. H. D.	*Ergonomics: functional design for the catering industry*	Edward Arnold, London, 1971
Tandy, C.	*Handbook of urban landscape*	Architectural Press, London, third impression 1975
Taylor, J.	*Fire Precautions Act in practice*	Architectural Press, London, 1977
Goldsmith, S.	*Designing for the disabled*	Architectural Press, London, 1976
	Building Regulations	HMSO, London, 1976

Acknowledgements

I am grateful to all those who have worked on this book with me, to the staff of the Design Council for their valuable editorial and graphic help, and to Peter Wilson of the Lygon Arms for his enthusiastic encouragement at the outset of the project.

I am also indebted to my colleagues for giving me the benefit of their knowledge and experience, and to the staff of my office for drafting illustrations and typing the text.

Lastly, I could not have completed the book without the assistance of many photographers, architects and designers who supplied illustrations.

PAGE	BUILDING	ARCHITECT/DESIGNER	PHOTOGRAPH
Cover and 3	Tower Hotel, London	Renton Howard Wood Levin Partnership	Henk Snoek
3	Restaurant, Leamington Spa	Douglas Smith Stimson Partnership	Douglas Smith
4	The Maltings, Beccles	Fielden & Mawson	Fielden & Mawson
	Turkey Cafe, Leicester	Original building by Arthur Wakerley	Leicester Polytechnic and Douglas Smith
5	Sveti Stefan Hotel, Yugoslavia	—	Douglas Smith
12	Hidcote Manor, Gloucestershire	—	Douglas Smith
13	Danish landscape	—	Peter Taylor
	Biba roof garden, London	—	Douglas Smith
15	Japanese garden, Expo	—	Douglas Smith
16 left	Inn on the Park, London	—	Douglas Smith
17	Katsura Imperial Villa Garden, Kyoto, Japan	—	Douglas Smith
18	Hidcote Manor, Gloucestershire	—	Douglas Smith
20	Details from Germany, Switzerland and England	—	George Perkins, Cement and Concrete Association
21	Courtyard, Zurich	E Baumann	F Maurer, SWB Zurich
23	Restaurant, St James's Park, London	Eric Bedford for the Ministry of Public Buildings and Works	George Perkins, Cement and Concrete Association
25	Health spa, Baden, Switzerland	—	George Perkins, Cement and Concrete Association